WS
745
App
Pamp

The National
Autistic Society

How to use this publication

This book is a brand new edition of a very popular NAS publication. There are many new approaches to autism and old entries have been thoroughly revised.

Approaches to autism is presented like a dictionary, with the entries appearing in alphabetical order. This is designed to make it clear and easy to use. For each approach there is a brief description and suggestions on where to go for further information.

Each entry has been written by someone who knows and uses the method, in some cases someone who has been involved in its development. Each contributor has described in about 300 words:
- the aims and expectations of their method
- what it involves in practical terms
- which individuals they believe it can help.

We would like to stress that in preparing this list we have tried to include everything without judging or discriminating. Inclusion does not mean that the NAS supports or recommends an approach. In the entries contributors express their own views in their own words. Our intention is to bring together and make available information which has previously been locked away in a lot of separate heads. We hope that it will help readers to make informed decisions and to choose a course of action appropriate to their own particular circumstances.

We are very grateful to all the contributors for their help and hard work in writing their entries and for the support of all the people and organisations who have agreed to be included in this list as contacts.

To help you with further research, we have marked (*) books which are available from NAS publications. www.autism.org.uk/pubs
Tel: 0845 458 9911
Fax: 0845 458 9912

This book is revised as new information comes in. If you find any inaccuracies or if you know of any other approaches which should be included, please let us know by writing to:

The Publications Department
The National Autistic Society
393 City Road
London EC1V 1NG
Tel: 020 7903 3595
Fax: 020 7833 9666
Email: publications@nas.org.uk

A question of judgement

Lorna Wing

Judging the efficacy of different approaches to the autistic spectrum is no easy task. It is helpful to see the problem in the context of the natural life history of these conditions.

The natural history of autistic conditions

People with autistic spectrum conditions (ASC) have a different pattern of brain development compared with others with a more typical developmental history. The differences are present from the very beginning of life. Typically developing babies seem to have an inbuilt intense interest in other humans and an equally intense desire to communicate. In contrast, babies with autistic conditions have little or no interest in people. Instead they find pleasure in physical sensations, movements and objects. This lack of interest in people is associated with delayed or absence of development of understanding of others' thoughts, feelings and needs, a lack of desire to please, and problems with communication.

People with autistic spectrum conditions find it hard to adapt to the demands of everyday life that are imposed by the sociable majority. This can result in refusal to conform to any demands, leading to what is termed 'challenging behaviour.' However, as with everyone, there are changes with development. The years between two and five can be particularly difficult for children with autistic conditions and their families but things tend to become easier from five or six up to around ten years of age. The teenage years may be turbulent because of the physical changes of adolescence. The problems may continue into the twenties or even the thirties but, in later adulthood, many people with autistic conditions have settled into a niche in life that suits them. Those who have autistic conditions in a subtle form and have average or superior levels of cognitive ability have the best chance of becoming fully independent adults. Many of the more able adults can use the positive skills and assets that go with autistic conditions to work in open employment and live independently.

In general, as they grow up, even those with the most marked form of autism tend to become less indifferent to people and develop social responsiveness on a simple level, especially towards their families and people they know well. However, the underlying neurological differences remain even though mitigated by maturation. They are shown in subtle form in the most able adults but they continue to be present throughout life.

In addition to the slow changes over the life cycle, people with autistic spectrum conditions can go through shorter-lived ups and downs in response to events in the environment or within themselves. It is against this background of varying phases with a general tendency to slow improvement over many years that the effect of any approach has to be judged. Since most of the available approaches need time to work, evaluating them requires a long-term view in a situation in which parents are desperate for immediate solutions to pressing problems. The difficulties are compounded by the fact that there are large variations in levels of ability, patterns of skills, responses to sensory input and personality and temperament among people with autistic conditions. For these reasons there are enormous differences in individual needs.

Aims of approaches

The aims of different approaches to autism can be classified into four basic types. First, organisation of the environment; second, modifying behaviour; third, teaching skills; fourth, attempts to 'cure' (that is, to make more typical) the underlying neurological and psychological differences from the typical patterns. Some approaches concentrate on one of these aims while others combine two or more.

The research studies that have been carried out have shown that some of the approaches that aim to make the environment more appropriate and/or to develop specialised educational techniques have helped people with autistic spectrum conditions to adapt better to everyday life and to learn useful new skills. The provision of a calm, structured and organised environment and a programme of education, occupation and leisure geared to the needs of each individual are the basic requirements for all those with autistic conditions. Many of the approaches in this book are, in effect, ways of achieving such an environmental and educational programme. Different techniques may suit different people – for example Low Intrusion Teaching may be the most suitable approach for some children whereas the intensity of the Higashi Daily Life Therapy may be too intrusive for them, though just right for others. Parents and professionals should,
ideally, discuss and work together to find the best type of programme for each individual child or adult.

Evaluating different approaches

When deciding if a particular approach is working for a child or adult, it is important not to rush to judgement. Starting a new regime may produce a temporary change (for better or for worse) which then settles back into the usual pattern after a varying length of time.

Judgements made in this initial period may have to be changed later on. As long as these complications are taken into account, it is possible to measure the results of any approach designed to improve skills and quality of life by comparing its effects with those of other techniques with the same aim, and with the outcome that would occur in the natural course of events. Studies carried out over a long period of time with matched groups of children are not easy to set up but are essential for valid assessments of the effects of any approach.

Much more difficult to assess are the methods that are aimed at 'curing' the underlying neurological and psychological differences in brain function. During the nearly 40 years in which I have been working in the field of autism, I have seen many 'treatments' come and go. These include medications, diets, psychotherapies, behavioural therapies and methods that can only be described as magical or mystical. They range from the plausible to the bizarre but, sadly, none has so far proved to be a cure. Parents of young children who have just been diagnosed as having an autistic condition are particularly likely to try anything that promises a cure, especially if they live in an area where there are few or no support services. It is in this type of situation that The National Autistic Society's EarlyBird Programme, offering support, realistic information and practical advice to small groups of parents of pre-school children, has proved so valuable. This programme has the added advantage of independent evaluation and continuing monitoring.

Changes in behaviour, such as increase in eye contact or willingness to be cuddled, have been claimed by some therapists as evidence of 'cure' but are not, in themselves, evidence of the disappearance of the underlying difficulties of social understanding. Equally dubious is the measurement of success in terms of the number of children attending mainstream school, since this depends upon skills and behaviour rather than any change in the underlying brain function. School placement is also affected by local administrative practices in relation to the education of children with special needs.

Scientific testing of any method said to 'cure' autistic conditions would require considerable knowledge of these conditions, expertise in designing such trials, adequate resources both of personnel and finance and real long-term commitment. Such resources are hard to come by because of competition imposed by other demands. They are likely to become available only for testing methods for which some convincing evidence exists that the effort would be worthwhile.

Some words of warning

In the present state of limited knowledge of the positive or negative effects of methods claimed to be treatments, some warnings need to be heeded.

1   Beware of therapists who state or imply that improvements cannot occur without the treatment they advocate. As already emphasised, most people with autistic spectrum conditions do show at least some improvement over time even without very specialised help. To be of any value a method must produce results that are significantly better than the improvements that occur naturally over the course of time.

2   Beware of the bias in results if only the more able children are accepted for treatment. It is these children who make the most progress without special help. It is possible to pick them out quite early in life and, if they are the only ones treated, the success rate is bound to be high.

3   Beware of the evaluation of results that are carried out by the therapists themselves, especially if they charge high fees. Assessments should be done by independent observers who can take an objective attitude.

4   Beware of those who assume that short-term improvements automatically lead to long-term benefits without producing objective evidence that this is the case.

5   Beware of treatments that cause the child discomfort, pain, distress, anxiety or fear.

6   Beware of the therapist who overtly or covertly blames the parents for their child's disabilities and who exerts moral blackmail to prevent the parent terminating the treatment.

7   Whenever possible, take the views of the child or adult concerned into account and give them the importance they deserve.

When considering ways of helping their children with autistic spectrum conditions, parents should think about the needs of the whole family – their other children and, not least, themselves. Promoters of some approaches encourage, even demand, that what they see as the needs of the child with autism are given priority over everyone else in the family. Of course, parents have to make up their own minds on these issues. But, after a lifetime of experience in the field, my feeling is that this does not make for a good quality of life – for the child or adult concerned or for the rest of the family. As with all things in life, a proper balance is most likely to achieve the best quality of life for the whole family.

Advocacy

Contributor: Caroline Hattersley, Head of Advice and Advocacy, The National Autistic Society

Advocacy means speaking or acting on one's own behalf or on behalf of others. Advocacy operates in many ways, from parents advocating for their children's education to volunteers and paid independent specialists advocating for those who lack the ability or confidence to speak for themselves.

Adult advocacy models range from volunteer based long term approaches, known as Citizen Advocacy, to short term crisis or issue based advocacy. These schemes usually cater for people with learning disabilities or mental health problems, although there are an increasing number of generic organisations. Many of these support people with autistic spectrum conditions. There is also a strong self-advocacy movement of people with learning disabilities and with mental health problems.

In certain specific situations people now have a legal right to advocacy, through the Mental Capacity Act (2005). An Independent Mental Capacity Advocate (IMCA) will be made available to people who lack the capacity to make a decision about serious medical treatment or provision of residence. Independent IMCAs will be available from January 2007.

The advocacy sector has also started to provide advocacy for people who are unable to instruct. This may be due to communication difficulties (people who don't use words for example) or capacity issues (the Mental Capacity Act also provides a framework for assessing capacity which is decision specific). People on the autistic spectrum may fall into either or both categories, so it will be interesting to see how this change opens up advocacy options to people with an ASD.

In recent years the importance of children's rights has been recognised. Many local authorities have established children's rights officers and advocates for children living in residential care.

The NAS runs an Advocacy for Education Service providing advice and support around educational issues and an Adult Advocacy Project which supports the diverse advocacy needs of adults with autism and Asperger syndrome by working with the independent advocacy organisations and local autism organisations.

Further reading

Atkinson, A. (1999) *Advocacy: a review*. Brighton: Pavillion Publishing

B. Gray and R. Jackson (2002) *Advocacy and learning disability.* London: Jessica Kingsley Publishers

www.actionforadvocacy.org.uk Provides up to date information on advocacy legislation and developments.

For more information contact:

Caroline Hattersley, Head of Advice and Advocacy, The National Autistic Society, 393 City Road, London EC1V 1NG

Tel: 020 7903 3760

Allergy induced autism (AiA)

Contributor: Rosemary Kessick, CEO AiA

AiA supports and promotes biomedical research into the cause and effect of auto-immune related autism. AiA was registered in the UK as a charity in 1997 and now maintains a wide membership of parents and professionals.

AiA provides help and information to anyone wishing to implement dietary intervention, based on scientific studies. Information is disseminated by a comprehensive resource booklet, which members receive on joining, together with quarterly newsletters. AiA also runs helplines staffed by experienced volunteers.

Seminars and conferences are held regularly to update audiences on latest medical and scientific progress together with practical sessions on how to implement and maintain the diet. Additionally AiA acts as a forum enabling the world's leading researchers in this field to collaborate.

The children and adults helped by AiA often display one or more of the following:
- hyperactivity
- sleep problems
- giggling/screaming for no apparent reason
- excessive thirst
- craving/dislike for certain foods
- hot and sweaty, especially at night
- history of glue ear
- eats non-foods eg earth, sand, paper, soap
- diarrhoea and/or constipation
- swollen tummy
- constantly breaking wind
- constant catarrh/runny nose
- inability to control temperature
- red ears and/or face
- dark shadows under the eyes
- pale skin, pasty face
- aches, cramps, tiredness
- allergy in the family (asthma, eczema, hayfever, migraine)
- gut disorders in the family (coeliac disease, Crohn's disease, ulcerative colitis, pernicious anaemia, autistic enterocolitis).

AiA always advises that a medical practitioner and dietician be consulted before implementing dietary intervention.

For more information contact
AiA Information, 11 Larklands, Longthorpe, Peterborough PE3 6LL
Tel and Fax: 01733 331771 | Email: aia@autismmedical.com | www.autismmedical.com

Anti-fungal treatments

Contributor: Paul Shattock, Autism Research Unit, University of Sunderland

For many years there has been believed to be a relationship between autism and yeast – largely *Candida* – infections. The exact relationship is uncertain but many parents and some professionals – mainly complementary – have used anti-fungal (yeast) programmes to ameliorate the symptoms of autism.

It may be that infections are the result of an impaired immune system and it has been argued that over-use of antibiotics in infancy could be responsible. Antibiotics are used to eliminate bacteria but doing this will always leave an opportunity for yeasts and other fungi to become established. *Candida* are the best known sources of these infections.

Testing for the infestation of these organisms is not easy because they inhabit the intestines of all of us. It is only when present in abnormal levels that they could be problematic but the precise method by which they could cause problems remains unclear.

In the context of the opioid excess theory of autism (see 'Gluten and Casein Free Diets') these infections could result in increased permeability of the intestinal wall. It has also been suggested that they could produce substances which inhibit the enzymes which break down peptides within the intestines. The consequences of either of these actions would be increased levels of potentially active peptides passing from the intestines into the blood stream. There are a number of interventions which may be used to reduce these infections. Nystatin is the drug employed in orthodox medicine for this purpose but a prescription is required and in the UK doctors are often unwilling to prescribe such substances without very good reason.

Natural products such as grape-seed oil and garlic oil may be beneficial. Many parents use **probiotics** as dietary supplements such as *Acidophillus* or *Lactobacillus* but it should be borne in mind that many such supplements have been prepared and stored so badly that these 'good bacteria' are effectively dead and so without value.

Yeasts thrive on sugar, particularly sucrose, and many parents cut down on sugars in an attempt to eliminate or reduce yeast infestations.

Published reports of effectiveness of these anti-fungal interventions are of the case-study type and so not convincing. However the numbers of parents and carers using such interventions is impressive. Certainly, along with other interventions, treatments to control yeast infestations should be considered.

For more information contact

The Autism Research Unit, School of Health Sciences, University of Sunderland, Sunderland SR2 7EE
Tel: 0191 510 8922 | Fax: 0191 567 0420 | Email:aru@sunderland.ac.uk
http://osiris.sunderland.ac.uk/aut-cgi/homepage
See The Sunderland Protocol

Applied Behaviour Analysis

Contributor: Kirsty Hayhoe MEd, BSc, DipHE, Peach Clinical Manager

Behaviour Analysis studies the impact of the environment on behaviour. ABA is the application of this science and has been used to help many areas of society, from traffic safety to the treatment of eating disorders. The education of children with autism is an area which has particularly benefited from the methodology. Its use is supported and validated by a wealth of scientific research.

ABA programmes for children with autism typically have two main components:
1. Skill-building: teaching the deficit behaviours (social interaction, communication, play skills etc)
2. Behaviour Management: decreasing behavioural excesses (self-stimulatory behaviours, non-compliance, aggression, rigidity etc).

A positive approach

Motivation and positive relationships are key: children learn best when they are having fun and this is always a priority.

One-to-one instruction

Initially, instruction is provided in a one-to-one setting (with one tutor and one student). This arrangement promotes attending skills and decreases the likelihood of the child becoming distracted. The child is gradually exposed to greater distractions with the ultimate goal of him/her learning within a group situation at school.

Intensity

Success in an ABA programme is generally considered to depend on the intensity of the programme. Early research by Dr Lovaas (1987) has shown that children receiving 40 hours per week of therapy evidenced significant gains in IQ scores and many were able to achieve successful mainstream school placements.

Early age of treatment onset

Another important variable in predicting success with ABA is the age of the child at the start. Research indicates that children who start treatment before the age of 42 months are likely to make the most gains. However, children at any age can benefit from ABA and recent studies have also demonstrated its effectiveness for school-age-children. (Elkeseth, et al, 2002)

Family involvement

Programmes typically start at home until the child is able to successfully interact socially with his/her peers. For maximum success to be achieved, family participation is critical.

For more information contact

Peach (Parents for the Early Intervention of Autism in Children)
The Brackens, London Road, Ascot, Berkshire SL5 8BE
Tel: 01344 882248 | Fax: 01344 882391 | Email: jacqui.wellbrook@ntlworld.com
Email: info@peach.co.uk; www.peach.org.uk

Aromatherapy massage

Contributor: Steve Solomons, aromatherapist

Aromatherapy massage can provide a meaningful context for the development of shared attention behaviours, including the use of eye contact, pointing, showing and giving for the social purposes of sharing an experience with others.

Interactive aromatherapy massage can help children to learn to trust, share, initiate and reciprocate interactions with others. It is also a form of non-verbal communication and can enable the development of positive interactions in a non-verbal and non-threatening way, assisting individuals to become more aware of other people as well as themselves. In order to relate to others, there needs to be human physical contact, attention and communication on an appropriate level. There must also be a good reason to relate and aromatherapy massage, particularly when viewed from an interactive perspective, can offer this reason to relate.

Aromatherapy massage may also offer parents (and siblings) an opportunity to spend time with the child with an ASD in a non-stressful environment, in which both understand the rules.

Fragrances, typically lavender due to its therapeutic properties, are detected in smell detectors on the inside of the nose, and each smell receptor conveys the information via the olfactory nerve into the limbic system of the brain. As this part of the brain is responsible for both the sense of smell and the sense of emotion, the process of smell-memory can trigger an emotion or experience previously associated with that particular smell. Fragrances can therefore be used to help reinforce learning experiences by assisting in long term recall and multi-sensory learning.

Recommended reading

Harris, B. and Lewis, R. (1994) 'Physiological effects of massage.' *International Journal of Alternative and Complementary Medicine*, 12, 2, pp 16-17

Longhorn, F. (1993) *Pre-requisites to learning for very special people*. UK: Orca Computers Ltd

McGee, J. J., Menaloscino, M. D., Hobbs, D. C. and Menousek, P. E. (1987) *Gentle teaching – a non-aversive approach to helping persons with mental retardation*. New York: Human Sciences Press

Sanderson, H. and Harrison, J. (1991) *Aromatherapy and massage for people with learning difficulties*. UK: Hands on Publishing

Solomons, S. (2005) Using aromatherapy massage to increased shared attention behaviours in children with autistic spectrum disorders and severe learning difficulties. *British Journal of Special Education*, 32, 3, pp127 – 137

Tisserand, R. (1988) *Aromatherapy for everyone*. London: Penguin

Van Toller, S. and Dodd, G. (1988) *Perfumery: The psychology and biology of fragrance*. London: Chapman and Hall

Art therapy

Contributor: Anne-Marie Kennedy, NAS Sybil Elgar School

'Art enables us to find ourselves and to lose ourselves at the same time.'
Thomas Merton

The desire to make images is innate in all of us. As children we attempt to make patterns or representations of the world around us, even though it is considered an activity beyond practicality.

Art in a therapeutic context can provide an insightful tool of communication, a statement in a non-verbal form. Art is a powerful instrument for individual expression and art work can be bridges or 'elastic locations' where we can communicate our ideas – leave our fingerprint.

Art is process orientated. It teaches us how to use objects and materials with a purpose. This in turn allows us to sequence co-ordination and fine motor control. We can both celebrate the handmade, its neurophysiological effect, while make meanings from everyday practices and interactions.

In addition, Prokofiev said that by exploring viscous material, it can help sort out chaos by the process of taming 'messy' materials as a source of stimulation.

Art used in a therapeutic setting can support both the containment and release of feelings: there are no mistakes and each piece of art work is received as a means of communication or expression. Not only does this encourage confidence. It can also foster greater independence of thought and expression.

Through this there can be a development of interpersonal skills, helping to build communication skills as a way of connecting meaning fully with the outside world and how we make sense of it.

Most importantly, art enables us to transform the ordinary into something fantastic. This simple philosophy can be applied to other areas in life – no matter how bad things get, there is always the chance they can improve or be transformed.

For more information contact
British Association of Art Therapists
Mary Ward House, 5 Tavistock Place, London WC1H 9SN
Tel: 020 7383 3774 | www.baat.org.uk

Auditory Integration Training

Contributor: Zelda Landau, the National Light and Sound Therapy Centre

The National Light and Sound Therapy Centre in London pioneered the use of AIT PLUS, a combination of Dr Berard's original Auditory Integration Training, together with Light Therapy and a Sound Modulation system based on the work of Dr Tomatis.

The philosophy behind the treatment is that children and adults with autism frequently have distorted hearing and this can block communication, limit speech and social interaction and cause temper tantrums. The treatment does not claim to cure autism but aims at retraining the hearing to disregard intrusive sounds. AIT PLUS is proving to be a useful weapon against some of the most distressing symptoms of autism.

The treatment consists of two half hour sessions daily over a period of two weeks using Dr Berard's Audiokinetron. It is suitable for children from the age of three. Auditory Integration Training itself is available elsewhere in the world but the combined AIT PLUS treatment is unique to the Centre.

AIT PLUS is non-invasive and pleasant. Being of short duration it is a useful first option before considering lengthy therapies. The Centre is a Registered National Health Provider and Health Authorities frequently fund treatment.

Since 1992 the Centre has treated over 800 children. Our statistics are based on the reports of parents & teachers who responded to our evaluation questionnaires several months after treatment. Of these

- 46 % reported a major improvement
- 24 % reported a good response
- 21.5% reported minor improvements
- 9 % reported no change
- In one study of 218 non-verbal children, 108 began speaking or started speaking more fluently after a course of AIT PLUS.

Dr Stephen Edelson and Dr Bernard Rimland, both world authorities on autism, are on the Board of Advisers. Three members of the Centre's staff were personally trained by Dr Berard.

For further information contact

The National Light and Sound Therapy Centre,
80 Queen Elizabeth's Walk, London N16 5UQ
Tel and Fax: 020 8880 1269 | www.light-and-sound.co.uk | Email: zl@light-and-sound.co.uk

Augmentative Communication

Contributors: Margaret Golding and Professor Stuart Powell, Centre for Autism Studies, University of Hertfordshire

Impairment of communication is part of the diagnostic criteria of autism. Communicative intent is lacking, particularly in the early years. Parents often note in retrospect that their child's early behaviours seemed designed to switch off communication rather than stimulate it. Significantly it is not just the development of language which is afterwards affected but also non-verbal means of communication eg eye contact, joint attention and pointing.

Ways of supporting communication are therefore needed. For example, where the use of spoken language provokes difficulties instead of understanding then language needs to be supported with visible forms of communication eg objects, pictures or symbols. In this sense a broad definition of Augmentative Communication is practices and programmes which support the act of communication.

A good starting point is using objects of reference and gesture to support communication together with the economic use of simple language by the adult. In addition there are established programmes for promoting and supporting communication for children with ASD.

- A widely used multi-modal approach in the UK is **Makaton** (Grove and Walker, 1990). This system was originally designed for people with learning and communication difficulties and is therefore very accessible. It uses iconic signs from British Sign Language and symbols which are simple line drawings, together with normal grammatical speech. The aim is to aid communication and develop speech wherever possible. Children with ASD tend to respond well to pictures, photographs and symbols.
- There are several other symbol systems favoured in schools. The **PIC** symbols which use a white on black image is one example of a system that has been found to be particularly effective with children with severe learning difficulties.
- The **Picture Exchange System** (PECS) – see entry in this book.

It is important to stress that whatever system of augmentative communication is used it is best seen as part of the process of educating the child with autism rather than an end in itself.

Further reading

Grove, N. and Walker, M. (1990) *The Makaton vocabulary: using manual signs and graphic symbols to develop interpersonal communication.* Camberley: MVDP

For more information contact

The Makaton Vocabulary Development Project, 31 Firwood Drive, Camberley, Surrey GU15 3QD

PIC: CD Rom-Loddon Comput pic, The Loddons School, Sherfield on Loddon, Basingstoke, Hants RG27 0JD

Befriending

Contributor: Claire Rintoul and Maureen Walters,
The National Autistic Society Befriending and Volunteering

The National Autistic Society (NAS) Befriending Scheme offers someone directly affected by an autistic spectrum disorder or a family member the opportunity to benefit from a one-to-one relationship with a volunteer befriender. This in turn can be a form of short-term respite to the family or carers of the individual.

All befriending schemes are organised locally and offer practical structure for recruitment, training and support for the volunteers. The NAS obtain references and CRB Disclosures before matching volunteers to a suitable family or individual. Each befriending scheme is supported by a trained volunteers co-ordinator. On-going training and support for the volunteers are also provided. Volunteers are encouraged to claim travel expenses.

Our volunteers are asked to give a couple of hours of their time a week and to commit to a minimum of a year. After a suitable match is found for the family, an agreement will be signed to clarify how often the befriender will visit and what kind of activities they will do together. Possibilities for activities are almost unlimited. They can range from taking a child to the park, an extra pair of hands on a shopping trip or sitting in the home watching television.

Volunteer befrienders can be either men or woman (minimum age 18) from any background. They do not need to be experts in autism, but we do look for people who are open-minded, reliable, willing to learn and sensitive to the needs of others.

For more information contact
The Volunteering Network, The National Autistic Society, Castle Heights,
72 Maid Marian Way, Nottingham NG1 6 BJ
Tel: 0115 911 3369 | Fax: 0115 911 3362 | Email: volunteers@nas.org.uk
www.autism.org.uk/befriending

Biomedical Interventions

Contributor: Chantal Sicile-Kira, author and parent

More emphasis is now placed on the connection between an individual's physical and neurological health. Many biomedical interventions have been developed and have shown promise with children affected by ASD whose metabolic systems may not be functioning properly. It may be that their systems are not processing essential nutrients properly, possibly because of a food allergy or intolerance, or a 'leaky gut' where the wall of the intestine does not do its job of keeping its contents separately from the bloodstream, or as a result of high levels of mercury or other toxic metals in the child's body.

It is possible to check for food allergies by adding and removing the suspected culprit from the person's diet and taking data, before and after, on their behavior. Essential nutrients can be tested in the same way. However there are specific tests and analysis that can be done that are more indicative of what is going on in the metabolic system.

Increasing emphasis is now given to the positive effects of these interventions on many individuals on the autism spectrum. Most current research and anecdotal evidence is based on younger children, yet adults and teenagers have reported benefits from some of these therapies, especially dietary treatments and megavitamin therapies. According to the Autism Research Institute founded by Dr. Bernard Rimland, more and more young children are being recovered from autism through the use of biomedical interventions, together with intensive applied behavior analysis (ABA) programme.

Biomedical interventions cover a wide range of non-invasive treatments worth trying, eg gluten/casein-free diet, to others that should be done only under the care of a knowledgeable health practitioner, eg methyl B-12 shots. Other biomedical interventions include megavitamin therapy, anti-yeast (fungal) diet, chelation, intravenous immunoglobulin (IVIG) therapy, secretin, enzymes and sulphate ions.

Some of these interventions have no side effects. Some are expensive, others are cheap. Some have empirical research to back them up, while others have only anecdotal reports. As for all treatments and therapies, parents should carefully investigate what makes sense to pursue based on their child's symptoms and the advice of a trusted and knowledgeable health professional.

Further reading
Pangborn, J.B. and Baker, S.M. 2005 *Autism: effective biomedical treatments*. Autism Research Institute, San Diego, Ca.

For more information contact
Autism Research Institute at www.autismwebsite.com/ari/dan/dan.htm

Boston Higashi School: Daily Life Therapy

Contributor: Ann S. Roberts, PhD

The Boston Higashi School in Randolph, Massachusetts, USA and the Musashino Higashi Gakuen in Tokyo, Japan, are the only two schools in the world to use the philosophy of Daily Life Therapy, developed by the late Dr. Kiyo Kitahara, for the education of children with Autism Spectrum Disorders.

The foundation of Daily Life Therapy consists of the three principles of vigorous physical exercise, emotional stability, and intellectual stimulation that together, without the use of psychotropic medications, help a student learn to establish and regulate his/her own biological rhythms in order to gain stamina, strength, physical coordination, mental awareness and alertness, and improvements in mood, thereby reducing anxiety, improving interpersonal relationships and leading to greater readiness to explore one's surroundings.

Based on this unique philosophy, at the Boston Higashi School, the Daily Life Therapy methodology is consistent across all aspects of teaching and campus life. Students are taught social education in group-dynamic classes that naturally foster interactions and relationships as they study a broad-based age and developmentally appropriate curriculum covering literacy, math, science, social studies and the arts, consisting equally of music, visual arts, physical education, and computer technology.

The Boston Higashi School serves both day and residential students with ASD diagnoses aged 3-22. The day programme is open 217 days and the residential programme runs 304 days.

Students participate in a variety of integrated and community programmes both day and residentially at all age levels. The transition class participates in an integrated pre-school. Elementary and high school age students participate in campus social mainstreaming or individually mainstream in public or private school settings and emergence students (aged 19-22) have paid employment education in the community. The residence uses all of the community resources for daily living and recreational activities.

We see the parent-teacher-child partnership as crucial to our mission. We sponsor guest speaker programmes and international conferences, make weekly calls and updates, encourage parents to visit and observe their child in class generally and to target specific areas in which to receive training, collaborate in setting vacation goals, make home visits (respite staff have visited internationally!) in person or by video and run sibling programmes as well as having an open special sibling email line for questions and concerns.

For more information contact:
Rosemary Littlefield, Executive Director, 800 N. Main St., Randolph MA, 02368, USA
Tel: 00 1 781 961 0800 | Email: littlefield@bostonhigashi.org

Brain Gym® and autism

Contributor: Buffy McClelland, Brain Gym Instructor

Brain Gym® is an eclectic technique that helps the brain and body work more effectively together. It uses specific physical movements to stimulate the development of new neural pathways. This improves learning difficulties (helping minimise problems arising from dyslexia, dyspraxia, attention deficit, and ASD), improves confidence, memory, concentration, organization skills, body coordination, chronic stress, phobias, and enhances performance in almost all areas of life. The technique was developed by Dr Paul Dennison in a decade-long experimental programme, where he determined which movements really do improve learning abilities.

Brain Gym practitioners find that Brain Gym movements which help improve brain communication between the rational frontal cortex and the emotional limbic system, and movements that improve the efficiency of sensory information filtering, are most beneficial for those with Autistic Spectrum Disorders. The Brain Gym technique is used successfully in some special schools specialising in ASD, and private Brain Gym Instructors from around the UK work with many children with ASD, helping improve interactions with other children, reducing emotional overwhelm and associated behavioural problems and improving academic performance.

How does Brain Gym work? Movement has profound and perhaps unexpected effects on connections between various parts of the brain. Human brains are designed to be flexible and to change throughout life. Physical movement is a very important key to enabling these changes to happen. Very early in life, even in the womb, movements stimulate the development of the brain. A baby automatically makes reflex movements in response to stimuli, and these automatic movements in turn stimulate the cortex of the brain (which is very undeveloped at birth) to create connections between brain cells. This interaction between body movement and the development of neural connections is retained as a life-long reaction, allowing the brain to be modified through controlled movements, even in adulthood.

Further reading

Dennison P. E. and Dennison, G., 1986. *Brain Gym: Simple activities for whole brain learning.* Ventura, Ca: Edu-Kinesthetics, Inc.

Dennison P. E. and Dennison, G., 1994. *Brain Gy : Teacher's edition revised.* Ventura, Ca: Edu-Kinesthetics, Inc.

Goddard, S. 2002. Reflexes, *Learning and Behaviour: a window into the child's mind.* Eugene, Oregon: Fern Ridge Press.

Hannaford, C., 1995. *Smart Moves : Why learning is not all in your head.* Great Ocean Publishers.

For more information contact
International Brain Gym Foundation www.braingym.org
UK Brain Gym Foundation Foundation | Tel: 020 8202 3141
www.braingym.org.uk | www.oxfordbraingym.com

Camphill communities and schools (Steiner)

Contributor: Rachel Mager, The Mount Camphill Community

Camphill is an international movement based on the philosophy of Rudolph Steiner. In Britain there are schools, further education colleges and adult villages. Permanent co-workers live in community together with people with disabilities and carry out the tasks of teaching, work in the house and on the land. Work in the villages is based on the land, housework and a variety of crafts.

In each Camphill centre there are people with many different forms of learning disabilities. Each is met as an individual with special needs and gifts and called upon to find their place in the community. All children, including those with autism, can benefit from living with others whose problems are different and may complement their own.

They can develop social relationships and find a dignity through learning and working together. The education in Camphill schools is based on the Waldorf (Steiner) curriculum. The children also have special remedial lessons and individual therapies as well as a range of artistic activities.

Some youngsters with autism are accepted into the Camphill colleges. However, it is evident that those who depend on a rigid discipline and structure to contain their difficulties are less likely to succeed than those who are able to cope with a freer social setting.

Further reading

Camphill Communities: Social Renewal through Community Living, available from The Mount Camphill Community, Wadhurst, East Sussex TN5 6PT
Tel: 01892 782 025 | Fax: 01892 782 917

For more information contact
Schools

(ages 6 to 16) Admissions Secretary, Sheiling School, Horton Road, Ashley, Ringwood, Hampshire BH24 2EB

Colleges

(ages 15 to early 20s)
The Mount Camphill Community, Wadhurst, East Sussex TN5 6PT

Villages

(adults)
Delrow College and Rehabilitation Centre,
Hilfield Lane, Aldenham, Watford, Herts WD2 8DJ

www.camphill.org.uk

Canine therapy

Contributor: Kari Dunn Buron, ASD Certificate Program, Hamline University, St. Paul, Minnesota

Research has shown many benefits of canine therapy. Some of the benefits mentioned are decreased stress, increased social interaction, increased motivation to participate, increased independence and increased communication. Research specific to ASD and canine therapy is extremely sparse. A 1989 report in the *Journal of Autism and Developmental Disorders* indicated that dogs could have a positive effect on children with autism. Washington State University has reported preliminary findings that provide tentative support for the use of Animal Assisted Therapy for children with ASD.

There are two titles for dogs working with children with autism: service dogs and therapy dogs.

A service dog works for an individual child and takes direction from the parent. In this model of intervention, a highly trained dog is harnessed to the child but is ultimately controlled by the parent who holds the leash. The goal of this therapy is to give the child more independence and access to the community. National Service Dogs of Canada is a leader in this form of canine support, with 10 years experience directly related to autism.

Follow-up surveys of families involved with service dogs report that they are able to go to grocery stores, restaurants and family gatherings without worrying about their child 'bolting' from the immediate environment. Video demonstrations of service dogs and their work with autism can be found on the NSD website.

The use of therapy dogs, or Animal Assisted Therapy, is most often characterised by a handler's use of his/her own highly trained dog to assist in educational or therapeutic settings. The training of these dogs is currently not regulated and varies greatly around the world. Training often follows traditional obedience with additional training to teach the dog to participate in specific therapeutic or classroom activities. The use of therapy dogs should be guided by educational goals and objectives addressing specific areas of need such as relaxation, relationship building, functional communication or increasing social motivation.

There is great potential in canine therapies but also a need for further research. Parents and professionals should approach the use of dogs in therapy with the caution and respect it deserves.

Further reading

Redefer, L. and Goodman, J. (1989) 'Brief report: pet-facilitated therapy with autistic children.' *Journal of Autism and Developmental Disorders,* 19(3), pp 461-467

Martin, F. (2001) *The effects of animal assisted therapy (dogs) on expression of pro-social behaviours in children with autism or other pervasive disorders.* Pullman WA: Washington State University http://www.petsforum.com/petcaretrust/PCTNR25.htm

For more information contact

National Service Dogs of Canada: www.nsd.on.ca/autism.htm
Hearing and Service Dogs of Minnesota: www.hsd.org
The Delta Society: www.deltasociety.org
Autism Service Dogs of America: www.autismservicedogsofamerica.com
Canine Partners UK: www.caninepartners.co.uk
Dogs for the disabled: www.dogsforthedisabled.org

Computer use

Contributor: Brendan Walsh, Educational ICT Advisor,
The National Autistic Society

Computers use offers a flexible, high status means of providing opportunities for people with autism in education, communication, creativity, leisure and employment. However it is important to bear in mind that computers alone do not provide a magic solution for people with autism, they may offer a range of very useful tools for a person with autism, but this must be embedded in a wider care and/or educational system to be effective. There is very little software written for people with autism. What is available may focus on one part of a person's autism (recognising people's facial expressions for example). There are often unrealistically high expectations of what a person with autism may achieve using a computer and it is important to be careful to choose systems that support and enhance someone's care, education or leisure rather than expect the computer to provide all of the aspects of one part of a person's life.

Computers do provide many opportunities for people with autism and are a vital part of many people's lives. Computers and the internet are credited by many in helping to create Autistic Communities. People with autism were able to use email (and later other technologies) to make contact and develop networks of people giving support, strength and a political voice to people with autism.

Computers provide a means of leisure that is considered acceptable in western society. Playing with a favourite box for hours on end isn't considered 'normal' by mainstream society, playing a computer game or surfing the web is.

Some people with autism have found that various computer based occupations have

allowed them to gain employment. From data entry to programming, there are people on the spectrum in a variety of IT occupations.

For some people with learning difficulties as well as autism, computers, together with aids such as switches, touch screens and interactive whiteboards, may provide a vital learning tool.

There is no single set of computer programs or equipment that will suit every person with autism. Questions such as: "what is the best software for people with autism?" are as unanswerable as "what are the best books for people with autism?" Each person with autism is an individual whose needs, interest and desires are different to everyone else in the world. The best sources of information are available online as these tend to be more up to date than printed material.

neurodiversity.com have a list of software for people with autism at:
http://neurodiversity.com/software.html

The same group have a list of computer resources for people with autism at:
http://neurodiversity.com/computers.html

The group 'Autsim and Computing' have a variety of resources that look at the theoretical and practical uses of computers for people with autism at:
http://www.autismandcomputing.org.uk/

The NAS keeps an updated fact sheet on computers at:
http://www.nas.org.uk/nas/jsp/polopoly.jsp?d=303&a=3276

Counselling

Contributor: Anja Rutten, Head of Social Programmes and Befriending, The National Autistic Society

Counselling is a form of talking treatment. It is also referred to as 'therapy' or 'psychotherapy'. Counselling offers individuals, couples or groups an opportunity to talk about what is problematic in their lives. It can be short-term or long-term, open-ended or time-limited, offered and paid for by the NHS or a private arrangement. Counselling can be used on its own or in conjunction with medication or other treatments.

There are many types of counselling and counsellors vary in their level of qualifications. The three main 'strands' to mainstream talking therapy are: cognitive-behavioural (also known CBT), humanistic (eg person-centred, transactional analysis, gestalt) and psychodynamic (eg psychodynamic, psychoanalytic). Some counsellors describe themselves as 'integrative,' which means they have integrated two or more approaches, or 'eclectic' which means they use other approaches and techniques in addition to their 'core' model.

At counselling sessions clients discuss their difficulties. This may be a specific problem or it may be more general. Counsellors do not usually give advice but help clients find their own solutions.

There currently is very little specific training for counsellors in how to work with clients with Asperger syndrome and knowledge of the condition and how it affects people is not common. It may therefore be necessary to compromise as the 'perfect' counsellor may not exist. It is, however, important to feel confident that the counsellor understands and that the client feels that the counselling process is helping.

When seeing a counsellor for the first time, it is important to discuss expectations, how the counsellor sees their role in the process and what they know about Asperger syndrome. If a counsellor is unwilling or unable to adapt their way of working to accommodate for the difficulties that people with Asperger syndrome may experience in the counselling relationship, which is largely dependent on verbal interaction, it may be best to try out another counsellor.

For more information contact

British Association for Counselling and Psychotherapy (BACP), BACP House, Unit 15, St John's Business Park, Lutterworth LE17 4HB
Tel: 0870 443 5252 | Email: bacp@bacp.co.uk | www.bacp.co.uk

UK Council for Psychotherapy (UKCP), 2nd floor, Edward House, 2 Wakley Street, London EC1V 7LT
Tel: 0207 014 9955 | Email: info@psychotherapy.org.uk | www.ukcp.org.uk

The British Psychological Society (BPS), St Andrews House, 48 Princess Road East, Leicester LE1 7DR
Tel: 0116 254 9568 | Email: enquiry@bps.org.uk | www.bps.org.uk

Dance movement therapy

Contributor: Chelsea Irwin, Laban Centre London

Dance movement therapy is the use of expressive movement and dance as a means for developing relationships and communication, reflection and emotional growth. Dance movement therapists are trained to understand meaning in movement. It is with this understanding that dance therapists try to engage with their clients, using their own bodies, movements, sounds and words. Empathy occurs not only through words, but also through supportive movement, fostering trust and the therapeutic relationship.

Verbal communication can be difficult for people with autism but dance movement therapy transcends the need for speech. A client's non-verbal communications – gestures, repetitive movements and body boundaries – are explored and examined in an accepting environment to encourage other patterns of relating.

Autism may manifest itself through difficulty with feelings. Dance movement therapists recognise that movement and emotions are interdependent and encourage their clients to explore a spectrum of movement qualities, from strong to soft and quick to slow, acknowledging the many possibilities that lie between two extremes. They attempt to link these bodily experiences with emotions, providing a safe outlet for the expression of feelings.

With increased body awareness and a sense of greater movement potential, clients feel more comfortable making choices and exploring alternatives to old routines. They begin to think beyond polarities to the possibilities which exist in between these and become better able to relate to and manage feelings.

Autism often contributes to a sense of isolation. Whether in groups or alone, dance movement therapy can engender a sense of belonging. One can communicate through movement what cannot be communicated through other social media. It is from this that a relationship of mutual trust, learning and respect grows.

Further reading

Parteli, L. (1995) 'Aesthetic Listening: Contributions of Dance/Movement Therapy to the Psychic Understanding of Motor Stereotypes and Distortions in Autism and Psychosis in Childhood and Adolescence,' *The Arts in Psychotherapy*, Vol. 23(3) pp.241-247

Erfer, T. (1995) 'Treating Children with Autism in a Public School System.' in Fran Levy (Ed.) *Dance and Other Expressive Art Therapies: When words are nor enough*, pp.191-211. London: Routledge

Economou, K. (1996) *Developing Interaction with an Autistic Child in Dance Movement Therapy.* Unpublished MA Dissertation. Laban Centre, London

For more information contact

Free Register of Dance Movement Therapists from: The Association of Dance Movement Therapy, c/o Quaker Meeting House, Wedmore Vale, Bedminster, Bristol BS3 5HX
E-mail: query@admt.org.uk

Detoxification and nutritional support in autistic spectrum disorders

Contributor: Dr. E.M. Danczak MB BS BSc Dip MedAc Dip OccH, Director, Manchester Centre

Complementary medicine practised in Manchester in the management of autistic spectrum disorders includes the use of homeopathy, complex homeopathy, nutritional support, probiotics and dietary management. This is supported by the use of specific laboratory investigation to assess detoxification function and mineral status.

The use of a strict treatment protocol using a balance of these medicines has proved helpful in the management of physical symptoms such as diarrhoea and constipation, reduction of infection and stabilisation of eczema or asthmatic episodes.

There is increasing evidence from our laboratory results that children with poor behavioural development settle down as their levels of minerals such as magnesium and zinc return to the normal range. The hyperactive, sleepless child begins to have a regular bedtime and, as behavioural ageing starts, the child picks up potty training and starts to produce vocal sounds. If language is already present they show an increase in vocabulary.

The disappearance of diarrhoea, a potent source of zinc loss, helped by the nutritional replacement and probiotics appears to be a good indicator for improvement of hyperactive behaviour and attention deficit disorder.

Zinc depletion occurs in 100% of children seen in the Manchester Clinic. Magnesium depletion is the second most common mineral deficiency, occurring in about 60% of children alongside zinc loss. Other minerals in deficit include manganese, chrome and selenium.

A disordered bowel flora is common in autistic children, with low populations of Lactobacillus and E.Coli. There is inappropriate overgrowth of certain bacteria such as Clostridium Difficile. This can be treated using probiotics, a mixture of bacteria, which have proved to be helpful.

Dietary intervention is used to relieve the pressure on the detoxification pathway involving Phenol sulphyltransferase, the poor function of which is indicated by sulphite in the urine. Removing foods with high phenolic content such as tomatoes and citrus fruit can be helpful in reducing hyperactive and ADD symptoms.

Food allergy testing by itself is not helpful in medium to long term management since restrictive diets without appropriate support can lead to malnutrition. In the short term exclusion diets have been shown to be helpful, particularly in the case of wheat and milk (see entry on gluten and casein free diet).

For more information contact
www.autismmanagement.com

Dimethylglycine (DMG)

Contributor: Paul Shattock, Autism Research Unit, University of Sunderland

There are many parents, particularly in the United States, who have found that DMG is helpful for their children. Some parents have reported quite dramatic improvements in language acquisition, mood and behaviour. There have been no scientifically valid trials which demonstrate efficacy but the anecdotal evidence is very considerable.

DMG occurs naturally in the human body and is involved in a number of significant biochemical reactions but it is not known which mechanism(s) are of relevance. It could, for example, have direct neurotransmitter action or it could be involved through its involvement in sulphur metabolism (cysteine to homocysteine conversions). It could be utilised for the formation of more complex molecules. There is a close relationship with trimethylglycine (TMG) and the two compounds are interconvertible. Interestingly, TMG – often sold under the name of 'Betaine' – has been available through health stores for at least 40 years for the treatment of hyperactivity. Some of the newer formulations contain both DMG and TMG. Products containing TMG tend to be considerably cheaper.

TMG is often used in the form of the hydrochloride where it will slightly increase the available hydrochloric acid and perhaps aid digestion.

Since DMG (and TMG) are normally found in the body, it is extremely unlikely that there could be toxic effects. Some parents have reported hyperactivity when using DMG but it is suggested that the addition of small amounts of folic acid will limit these problems.

Although concrete evidence of usefulness is scarce, the anecdotal evidence is considerable. These reports suggest that some 30% of children with autism will benefit from DMG but many parents feel that the benefits are comparatively transitory. Some parents reserve its use for particular occasions whereas others use it constantly.

For more information contact

The Autism Research Unit, School of Health Sciences, University of Sunderland, Sunderland 5RT 3SD
Tel: 0191 510 8922 | Fax: 0191 5670420 | Email: aru@sunderland.ac.uk
http://osiris.sunderland.ac.uk/autism
See The Sunderland Protocol

The Dore programme

Contributor: Julia Butcher, NAS Autism Helpline

The Dore programme is based on the theory that many learning difficulties are the result of a delay in the development of part of the brain called the cerebellum. The Dore programme supports recently emerging evidence that the cerebellum is not only responsible for motor control and balance but also has a role in the higher 'cognitive' functions of the brain such as learning and language.

The Dore programme tests the function of the cerebellum in three ways:
- posturography – looks at the cerebellum's function in terms of balance
- ocular-motor testing – looks at cerebellum's function in terms of the fine motor control used when tracking a stimulus with the eyes
- basic neurological testing of primitive reflexes which should disappear as the cerebellum is fully developed.

If these tests show a delay in the development of the cerebellum, a doctor will diagnose Cerebellar Developmental Delay (CDD). A set of simple physical exercises are then prescribed for each individual which stimulate the cerebellum, thereby increasing its function.

The exercise programme lasts on average between 12 and 18 months but this may be longer for those with severe difficulties. The individual is required to do the exercises twice daily, returning to the centre every six weeks for retesting and new exercises. This continues until cerebellar function has reached its potential – shows no more improvement. At this stage the person can complete the programme and should no longer be required to continue with exercises.

The Dore programme was developed by Wynford Dore in Warwickshire in response to his daughter's learning difficulties. It was first targeted at people with dyslexia, dyspraxia and ADHD and the company has published research to do with these conditions on their website. People with an ASD are accepted on the programme if they show a delay in the development of their cerebellum. However, no research has been published as yet with regards to the progress of individuals with an ASD, although subjective changes are reported.

Further reading

Parmeggiani, A., et al (2004) Pervasive developmental disorders and cerebellar malformations: literature review and personal cases, in: *Focus on autism research*, Ryaskin, O.T. (2004). New York: Nova Biomedical Books

Schmahmann, J. D. (1997) The cerebellum in autism: clinical and anatomical perspectives in: Bauman, M.L. & Kemper, M.D. *The neurobiology of autism*. Baltimore: John Hopkins University Press

For more information contact
Dore Centre
Tel: 0870 737 0017 | Email: info@dore.co.uk | www.dore.co.uk

Drama and movement therapy

Contributor: Lesley Bester, Drama and Movement Therapist

Drama and movement therapy can be beneficial for people on the autistic spectrum as it provides a non-confrontational space where individuals can express themselves safely through the medium of movement, drama and play.

Drama and movement therapy explores different ways of communicating which can be particularly useful for people who are non-verbal. Hearing and responding to the individual's 'voice' can bring about a sense of empowerment.

Safe expression of emotional difficulties contained within the art form is encouraged. Sometimes challenging behaviour can be channelled into creative movement expression.

Some of the work involves assisting the individuals in accessing their own creative potential. For some people on the spectrum this may be challenging as it can require symbolic understanding. The work in such a case would focus on finding other means of expression.

Using sensory and projective play the individual is assisted in building relationships with people through objects. Developing the ability to trust others and interact positively with people is one of the predominant aims, while always respecting the individual's choice to be who they are.

For more information contact

The Sesame Institute, 27 Blackfriars Road, London SE1 8NY
Tel: 020 7633 9690 | E-mail: sesameinstituteuk@btinternet.com
www.btinternet.com/~sesameuk

The British Association of Drama Therapists, 41 Broomhouse Lane, London SW6 3DP
Tel: 020 7731 0160
www.badth.ision.co.uk

Drug based approaches

Contributor: Dinah Murray

No psychoactive drug 'cures' autism: some may reduce some unwanted behaviour; all may have adverse effects of which some may be irreversible. It is advisable to use such drugs for short periods at very low doses, if at all. After longer periods withdrawal may be problematic and should be gradual.

Serotonin regulation is unusual in autism and many psychoactive drugs directly or indirectly affect serotonin. Nobody claims full understanding of these processes. Antidepressants like fluoxetine and paroxetine (SSRIs) and the antianxiety drug buspirone, boost circulating serotonin and may increase sociability and have a calming and cheering effect on some people. In some cases SSRIs steeply reduce stereotypical behaviours but in others may increase hyperactivity and aggression, worsen sleep patterns and initiate suicidal thoughts. They can also cause problems with urination and defecation and decrease sexuality.

Atypical antipsychotics olanzapine and risperidone alter both dopamine and serotonin regulation. In very low doses they may reduce aggression and self injury and promote social behaviour in some children and adults with autism. Dramatic weight gain and loss of sexual definition may rapidly occur with both atypical and typical antipsychotics like haloperidol, chlorpromazine (Largactil) and thioridazine (Mellaril). The worst antipsychotic effects are (rarely) sudden death, and (at around 5% per year, ie 20% after 4 years) tardive dyskinesia (TD), a severe frequently irreversible movement disorder. Other common distressing effects include tremors, continence problems, affective and cognitive blunting, extreme motor restlessness and despair. Apart from weight gain (and, perhaps, sudden death) most adverse effects are rarer with atypicals, especially from an eighth to at most a half of the standard lowest antipsychotic dose – autism is not a psychosis!

Opiate antagonist naltrexone may break addictive behaviour patterns involved in self-injury. Anti-epilepsy medications valproic acid and carbamazepine are sometimes prescribed to stabilise mood and reduce aggression, as is lithium. Both the latter require regular blood monitoring and long term lithium use promotes incontinence.

Betablockers also reduce aggression in some people and require regular blood-pressure monitoring. Ritalin (methylphenidate) may reduce hyperactivity in a small proportion of children with autistic spectrum disorders. Its main drawbacks are dependency and potential long term personality problems.

Further reading
Stahl S.M. (2000) *Essential Psychopharmacology*. Cambridge: Cambridge University Press

For more information contact
MIND has specialised knowledge on these drugs: 020 8519 2122 ex 275 (Mon-Fri 9.15-5.15))
APANA (Autistic People Against Antipsychotic/Neuroleptic Abuse) provides support and information to survivors and their carers: Chair: David N. Andrews; Patron: Wendy Lawson. c/o 1 Oak Tree House, Redington Gdns, London NW3 7RY
E-mail: Apana2000@hotmail.com | www.apana.org.uk

Facilitated Communication

Contributor: Dr Andy Grayson, Senior Lecturer in Developmental Psychology, Nottingham Trent University and Dr Anne Emerson, Research Fellow, Nottingham Trent University.

Facilitated Communication (FC) is an augmentative and alternative communication (AAC) strategy which is used by people with communication impairments and difficulty with pointing independently, including some people with autism. It involves a facilitator resisting the forward movement of the FC user when they are pointing by holding their hand or arm. . Often the pointing takes the form of typing on a keyboard. The physical support offered may help some people with autism to compensate for movement disorders, and/or difficulties with high level 'executive' control of action, including planning, staying on task, and inhibiting irrelevance.

The facilitator is an active partner in the interaction, giving on-going feedback, encouragement and emotional support to the FC user. However, the physical contact between the communicating partners means that there is a danger of the facilitator inadvertently influencing the pointing. A number of controlled studies published in the 1990's showed that this can happen, and most peer reviewed research papers to date have concluded that the emergent communications are really being authored by the facilitator, rather than by the FC user. More recent research has indicated that FC users are at least partly responsible for the communications produced.

Supporters of FC suggest that experimental studies only tell part of the complex story. They cite case histories and research papers where it has been found to be effective. For example, there are now a number of individuals who have achieved independent typing. Others need only minimal support, perhaps with a facilitator gently touching their shoulder or simply sitting near them. Nevertheless independence is very difficult to achieve and most FC users require on-going physical support whilst pointing.

The key prerequisites for anyone starting FC include:

- an understanding of the controversy surrounding its use and the dangers of inadvertent facilitator influence
- proper speech and language therapy advice from a suitably qualified professional, including a thorough assessment of independent communication skills
- a commitment to use FC alongside other communication strategies
- multiple facilitators available to encourage real, everyday communication, and to assist in on-going evaluation of the usefulness of the strategy for the FC user
- clear procedures for assessing the validity of any communication from the FC user which requires action or prompts some kind of change in their life
- an immediate and continued focus on teaching independent communication skills.

For more information contact

Dr Andy Grayson and Dr Anne Emerson, Division of Psychology, Nottingham Trent University, Burton Street, Nottingham NG1 4BU

Email: andy.grayson@ntu.ac.uk; anne.emerson@ntu.ac.uk

Gastrointestinal problems in autism spectrum disorders

Contributor: Brenda O'Reilly, Chair, Autism Unravelled

There can be no doubt that disturbances of the digestive system contribute to autism in a major way.

There is now documented evidence from Dr Andrew Wakefield of the Royal Free Hospital, London, that there are gross abnormalities in the gut wall of many people with autistic spectrum disorders. He associates these with the MMR – measles, mumps and rubella – vaccine.

The research of Paul Shattock at the University of Sunderland and Dr Kalle Reichelt in Norway shows that there are increased levels of peptides (breakdown products) from both gluten and casein – wheat and milk – in the urine of people with autism. This means that these substances are crossing the gut wall and getting into the blood stream.

Research by Dr Rosemary Waring at Birmingham University indicates altered levels of sulphate in people with autism. Sulphate lines the gut wall and keeps it slippery and intact.

Reports of parents and individuals with autism indicate frequent problems with severe diarrhoea and/or constipation, together with extreme abdominal discomfort, swollen tummy and excessive wind. Children with autism may be 'picky' eaters and sometimes they refuse to eat at all. They may eat erratically or snack all the time instead of eating full meals. Food can pass undigested into their stools. These can range from small pellets like rabbit droppings to very large blocks which are difficult to flush away or may resemble water or porridge. Stools can be of many colours, from yellow to very dark brown. Such children are also very thirsty and constantly in need of a drink.

Parents and carers often report that autistic behaviour worsens when certain foods are ingested and yet there is an abnormal craving for the very foods that cause the problems. Food may contain both synthetic and natural chemicals such as colouring and flavouring which cannot be properly broken down due to an under-active detoxifying system. These chemicals then build up and affect the brain.

Many other physiological and biological systems are affected in autistic spectrum disorders such as nutrition and the immune and detoxification systems.

For more information contact
Brenda O'Reilly, Autism Unravelled, 3 Palmera Avenue, Calcot, Reading, Berkshire RG31 7DZ
Tel and Fax: 0845 22 66 510 | Email: info@autism-unravelled.org
Website: www.autism-unravelled.org

Gentle Teaching

Contributor: Elinor Harbridge, Editor, Community Living

Gentle Teaching was developed some 20 years ago at Nebraska University by John McGee, Dan Hobbs and colleagues in response to what they saw happening to people whose behaviour was labelled as challenging. They called it the 'revolving door' syndrome. People were admitted to institutions, subjected to a behavioural modification programme and then discharged, their behaviour duly modified.

However, soon they were back in the same institution with even more challenging behaviour and subjected to even severer modification methods. At the time devices such as cattle prods and acid sprays were not uncommon. Today in the UK devices like control and restraint, time out and withdrawal of privileges or treats are still in frequent use. The unequal power struggle continues.

Proponents of Gentle Teaching regard such methods as dehumanising for both people and carers. However, if we regard a person's behaviour as an attempt to exert power over their circumstances we can imagine a different scenario, in which the person participates voluntarily in more rewarding human interactions.

The teacher focuses not on the person's behaviour but on the individual as a person. This means the teacher adopting positive human values in relation to the person and accepting the need to change their own behaviour in order to develop a relationship and achieve a fairer balance of power. It is a process of teaching that a person can influence others and the environment by less alienating methods.

Gentle Teaching requires the teacher to engage closely with the person using a simple task while maintaining a safe position. In Gentle Teaching the initial task is as simple as possible to maximise the opportunities for participation and praise. Careful observation of videoed interactions is used to discover the dynamic of the relationship between teacher and person so the latter can adapt their actions: a tiny movement, the tone of voice, the teacher's body position may all be significant.

Gentle Teaching has no set formula or hierarchy of rewards. Teachers use all their human understanding and skills to find the person and develop and sustain a rewarding relationship.

For more information and a training pack contact
Elinor Harbridge, Orchard House, Wootton Courtenay, Minehead, Somerset TA24 8RE
Tel and Fax: 01643 841 101 | Email: elinor.harbridge@virgin.net

Gluten – and Casein-free (GFCF) Diet

Contributors: Paul Shattock, Paul Whiteley, Lynda Todd
Autism Research Unit, University of Sunderland

Diets devoid of foods containing gluten (the primary protein found in wheat, barley and rye) and casein (milk and dairy produce) have for several years been reported to be helpful in ameliorating some of the core and secondary symptoms of autism (Knivsberg et al, 2001; Millward et al, 2004). There have been several published reports of open trials of such interventions, suggestive of positive changes in areas such as social interaction, attention, motor and language skills (Whiteley et al, 1999) combined with accompanying changes to co-morbid somatic problems such as abnormal bowel habits for a proportion of people on the autistic spectrum.

Specific predictive indicators of good outcome have yet to be formally finalised, although several factors are thought to be associated with successful results including:
(i) chronological age (young children often do much better on this type of intervention),
(ii) children exhibiting signs of self-injurious behaviours,
(iii) children showing overt signs of a high pain tolerance,
(iv) children who are more severely affected with autism and
(v) children presenting with corresponding problems with functional bowel habits (constipation and/or diarrhoea) (Afzal et al, 2003).

The development of the 'opioid-excess theory' provided an initial explanation as to why such dietary interventions may be useful for autism (Shattock and Whiteley, 2002). The suggestion that digestion of proteins such as gluten and casein may be inhibited combined with indications of abnormal permeability of specific membranes throughout the body allowing greater passage of biologically active break-down peptides with opiate (morphine-like) activity into the Central Nervous System (CNS), forms the basis of the 'intolerance' theory. More recent research suggests that such compounds may also have the ability to interact with the immune system indicative of an altogether more complex picture (Vojdani et al, 2003).

Success using this type of intervention is by no means certain. In some cases the benefits may not justify the efforts involved. These interventions are not problem-free and it is strongly advised that people considering them should seek professional, medical support prior to adoption of the diets.

References

Afzal N. Murch S. Thirrupathy K. Berger L. Fagbemi A,. Heuschkel R. (2003) Constipation with acquired megarectum in children with autism. *Pediatrics* 112: 939-942

Knivsberg A.M. Reichelt K.L. Nødland M. (2001) Reports on Dietary Intervention in Autistic Disorders. *Nutritional Neurosciences* 4: 25-37

Millward C. Ferriter M. Calver S. Connell-Jones G. (2004) Gluten- and casein-free diets for autistic spectrum disorder. *Cochrane Database of Systematic Reviews*: CD003498

Gluten – and Casein-free (GFCF) Diet (continued)

References (continued)

Shattock P. Whiteley P. (2002) Biochemical aspects in autism spectrum disorders: updating the opioid-excess theory and presenting new opportunities for biomedical intervention. *Expert Opinion of Therapeutic Targets* 6: 175-183

Vojdani A. Pangborn J.B. Vojdani E. Cooper E.L. (2003) Infections, toxic chemicals and dietary peptides binding to lymphocyte receptors and tissue enzymes are major instigators of autoimmunity in autism. *International Journal of Immunopathology & Pharmacology* 16: 189-199

Whiteley P. Rodgers J. Savery D. Shattock P. (1999) A gluten-free diet as an intervention for autism and associated spectrum disorders: preliminary findings *Autism* 3: 45 – 65

Further reading

Autism Research Unit, University of Sunderland (http://osiris.sunderland.ac.uk/autism)

*Jackson L. (2001) *A user guide to the GF/CF diet for autism, asperger syndrome and AD/HD.* London: Jessica Kingsley Publishers.

*Le Breton M. (2001) *Diet intervention and autism: implementing the gluten free and casein free diet for autistic children and adults – a practical guide for parents.* London: Jessica Kingsley Publishers.

Growing Minds

Growing Minds is an integrative approach to ASDs in which parents are trained and supported to meet their child's social, educational and biomedical needs through individualized programs, tailored specifically for the child. Growing Minds integrates educational, play-based, relationship-oriented, behavioural, biomedical and sensory methods. Parents and professionals receive training and ongoing support to work with children at home and school through a variety of services, including intensive training in Florida, long-distance consultation by phone, video and internet and seminars in the UK.

Director Steven Wertz has 24 years of experience in training parents to support and educate children with autism. Steven is a Board Certified Behavior Analyst (also known as ABA, DTT and Lovaas training) who has worked individually with over 1,000 children with ASDs. Prior to establishing Growing Minds in 1998, Steven taught for fifteen years in the Son-Rise Program. As the only individual to have earned certification in both Behavior Analysis and Son-Rise, Steven is uniquely qualified to integrate the best of both approaches.

Typical program benefits include increasing motivation, attention and cooperation; improving communication and language; increasing social interaction, eye contact, affection and enjoyment of people; reducing challenging behaviours; and improving cognitive, academic, motor and self-help skills. Growing Minds programs are customized and targeted for the needs of individuals at every age and every ability level. Parents receive a free Initial phone consultation.

For more information contact
The Growing Minds Autism Program
15096 115th Avenue North, Jupiter, Florida 33478, United States
Tel: 00 1 561 748 9697 | Fax: 00 1 561 748 6543 | Email: info@autism-programs.com
www.autism-programs.com

The Hanen program for parents of children with ASD: More Than Words

Contributor: Elaine Weitzman, Hanen Centre, Toronto

This is a group training programme for parents of pre-school children with autistic spectrum disorders, developed by The Hanen Centre, a Canadian charity. It teaches parents how to foster social interaction and language learning in ways that have been shown to help children with autistic spectrum disorders – eg breaking activities into small steps, providing repetition and structure, using visual supports and engaging in high-interest interactions in which the child learns while having fun.

Over a three-month period about eight families in a More Than Words program attend a series of eight classes led by a Hanen-trained speech and language therapist (SLT). Here parents learn to understand their children's unique learning style and to identify their stage of communication development. Some may be non-verbal, while others may be able to carry on short conversations. Through interactive and practical activities, supplemented by the More Than Words teaching videotape, parents learn to use strategies that have been shown to help children with autistic spectrum disorders communicate in more mature and conventional ways.

Families also participate in three video feedback sessions with the Hanen SLT, during which parent and child are videotaped, with the parents applying the strategies learned in the classes. The SLT provides on-the-spot coaching and then the parents and the SLT review the videotape together. They identify what is working well and what the parent can change to help facilitate the child's social communication and language learning.

The content of the program is outlined in a user-friendly, beautifully illustrated guidebook called More Than Words. Parents can use the guidebook to review what they have learned in the classes as well as to find some new ideas.

Currently 30 of the 1,500 Hanen SLTs in the UK are trained to lead More Than Words programs, with more training workshops for Hanen SLTs to be offered across the UK.

For more information contact

Anne McDade, Coordinator, Hanen UK/Ireland, 9 Dungoyne Street, Maryhill, Glasgow G20 0BA
Tel: 0141 946 5433 | Email: uk_ireland@hanen.org

Fern Sussman, More Than Words Program Manager, The Hanen Centre, Suite 403 – 1075, Bay Street, Toronto, ON NSS 2B1, Canada
Tel: 00 1 416 921 1073 | Fax: 00 1 416 921 1225 | Email: fern@hanen.org

Homeopathy

Contributor: Annie Hall MCPH, RSHom, homeopath specialising in children with learning, behavioural and developmental problems

Homeopathy is different from any other type of medicine. A homeopath is interested in what makes you you. Why you think you have the problem you have at present?

Many questions will be asked before the homeopath chooses the most appropriate remedy for you. So for instance there is no one remedy prescribed for autism as each person has a different way of exhibiting their problem, even within the same family. What is needed is detailed knowledge of the patient and how he/she responds to life's problems.

When choosing your remedy, the homeopath will look at your physical, mental and emotional problems all together. As these are all things that affect YOU, so they are all of equal importance. The more knowledge the homeopath has the better, to be able to chose the most suitable remedy.

There are over 3,500 remedies available and the list grows all the time. Many remedies are made from plant material, others however come from metals and even substances such as snake venom. All are given in a form that is very unlikely to do any harm. They are taken as tiny tablets to be sucked, making them ideal for even very young children. They can be taken alongside conventional medicine or, as is often the case, as a first line of treatment. The remedies can be used for acute problems such as ear ache, or more chronic ones such as temper tantrums.

Homeopathy has been used safely for over 200 years all over the world, and the remedies are chosen to help the Vital Force heal the individual from within. One analogy that I like is that it helps get the radio dial back on station. Therefore often it only needs a small tweak but at other times a larger one will be needed.

In an appointment there is time taken to listen to all the implications. There is continuity of care and, best of all, there is the likelyhood that the remedy will help you.

Further reading

Ullman J.R., Ullman R. and Luepker I. (2005) *A drug free approach to Aspergers syndrome and autism*. Edmonds, WA: Picnic Point Press

Lansky A. (2003) *Impossible cure: the promise of homeopath*. Portola Valley, CA: R.L.Ranch Press

For more information contact:
The Society of Homeopaths
Tel: 0845 450 6611 | www.homeopathy-soh.org

Intensive interaction

Contributor: Phoebe Caldwell

We find it difficult to get in touch with children and adults on the autistic spectrum, especially those who are non-verbal. Intensive Interaction addresses these problems by using people's language to establish emotional engagement. Starting with extremely careful observation, it looks at what the individual is doing, how they are 'talking to themselves.' What it is that has significance for them and engages their attention? Do they make sounds (these may be as small as those made in the breathing rhythm) or movements (flap hands) or use special rhythms? Are they particularly focused on a special activity such as tearing paper or turning light switches on?

Intensive interaction works by joining in those initiatives that are already part of their repertoire. It answers rather than mimics, using elements of their 'language' that their brain recognises. The brain very quickly recognises its own sounds or movements and attention is shifted from solitary self-stimulation to shared activity. We use our responses to empathise. Practitioners do not find it necessary to use a dedicated room since the brain so quickly recognises its own language. Partners quickly learn that if they make an initiative they will receive an answer that has meaning for them, a vital step in leaning to communicate. Using body language in this way was introduced in Britain by the psychologist, Geraint Ephraim in 1986. It is now used widely in schools and services, and abroad, particularly in Denmark and Australia.

Normal outcomes are relaxation, an increase in social responsiveness, a decrease in distressed and challenging behaviour. Parents say, 'our children are happier.' Teachers and therapists say it enables them to make more effective contact with their children. Intensive Interaction is equally effective with adults.

Further information can be obtained from the following sources:

Further reading

Nind, M. and Hewett, D. ( ) *A practical guide to intensive interaction.* Kidderminster: BILD

Caldwell, P. and Hoghton, M. (2000) *You don't know what it's like.* Brighton: Pavilion Press

Caldwell, P. (2002) *Learning the Language.* Brighton: Pavilion Press (Training video)

*Caldwell, P. (2006) *Finding you finding me.* London: Jessica Kingsley Publishers

Caldwell, P. 'Can we talk?' (autism) and 'Speak to me' (intensive interaction) Free simple introductory handouts on www.nwtdt.com (under Publications)

Caldwell, P. (Due March 2007) *From isolation to intimacy.* London: Jessica Kingsley Publishers

For more information contact
www.intensiveinteraction.co.uk
Phoebe Caldwell: Email: phoebecaldwell@btopenworld.com
Concept Training
Tel: 01524 832 828

Internet Communities

Contributor: Brendan Walsh, Educational ICT Advisor,
The National Autistic Society

The advent of common access to the internet in the first world created opportunities for people with autism to form autistic communities in ways that had not previously been available. For the purpose of this article, internet communities are defined as groups of people who communicate or interact using the internet. Web sites that are effectively one way communication are not included. Email lists, messageboards, social networking and virtual worlds are included.

Online communities originally started as e-mail lists, as that was the only technology available at the time, but as web based technologies such as chatrooms and message boards arrived, these were also used.

Some of the online communities have developed to encompass the offline world as well. For example, the group Aspies for Freedom launched the Autistic Pride Day, when events are held around the world and Autism Network International launched the Autreat ASD friendly conferences in 1996.

Communities come into existence, merge, change and disappear over time so the best place to get up to date information is on the internet. Below are links to some of the communities that currently exist, as well as to information sources that may provide further links. Things do go out of date very quickly as servers move, internet companies change and people get bored and so this information is just to get you started.

Email groups, message boards and chatrooms
Wrong Planet is a web community for individuals with ASDs and their parents that host chatrooms and forums: http://www.wrongplanet.net/

The Autism Network International host a email group, the details of which can be found at: http://ani.autistics.org/ani-l.html

Independent Living on the Autistic Spectrum host email groups in English, Dutch and Swedish, details at: http://www.inlv.demon.nl/

Asples for Freedom host autism forums, Aspergers forums, and an autism chat room at: http://www.aspiesforfreedom.com/

There are hundreds of autism related email groups hosted by 'Yahoo! Groups', the vast majority for parents. Some of these groups are dormant, even if they have thousands of members; a good way to check that there anything going on is to check the "activity In last 7 days" of the group at its homepage (you can do this without subscribing). These can be searched at: http://groups.yahoo.com

ChatAutism has chatrooms for people with autism, people with aspergers, as well as parents.
http://www.chatautism.com/

Virtual Worlds
There is an autistic space on Second Life at:http://slurl.com/secondlife/Porcupine/37/185/105/ and others may well follow.

Links
Autistic Culture have a links page with lots of online communities listed at: http://www.autisticculture.com/

The Autism Network International has links to a variety of communities and other resources at: http://ani.autistics.org/other_autism.html

Irlen Syndrome

Contributor: Tina Yates, Irlen East, UK

People with Irlen Scotopic Sensitivity Syndrome have sensory perceptual problems that can affect the way the brain interprets what is seen and therefore how individuals interact with the world around them. 70 % of the information which an individual receives comes in through the eyes and therefore any problem in the way the brain processes visual information can cause difficulties in the general ability to function.

The types of sensory perceptual deficits associated with autism are unique. As a result people with autism may experience the following:
- alienation
- poor concentration
- poor social skills
- low self-esteem
- system overload
- poor body awareness
- sensory compensation
- Incomplete or faulty information

Preliminary results indicate that some individuals suffering from sensory perceptual distortions may be helped by the Irlen Method which uses a patented treatment utilising colour filters worn as glasses to reduce or eliminate perceptual difficulties. The colour seems to change the rate at which the information is processed by the brain allowing it to:
- correctly match up information
- sort the information
- process information.

Changes result in:
- integration of the senses
- improved perception
- ability to respond
- body awareness
- spatial awareness
- eye contact
- communication
- self control.

For more information contact
Irlen East, 4 Park Farm Business Centre, Fornham St Genevieve, Bury St Edmunds, Suffolk IP28 6TS
Tel and fax: 01284 724 301 | Email: tina@irleneast.com | Website: www.irleneast.com

The Listening Program®

Contributor: Alan R Heath, Brain Gym® Instructor, UK TLP Trainer, Consultant and Educational Trainer

It is well known that people with autism often have associated auditory processing difficulties. These can include, but are not limited to:

- hypersensitivity to sound
- difficulty understanding speech in background noise
- problems with sound discrimination
- challenges with acquiring and processing speech sounds and language.

The Listening Program (TLP) is a music-based auditory stimulation method that trains the brain to improve the auditory skills needed to effectively listen, learn and communicate.

Listening also helps facilitate better integration and organisation in the sensory and motor systems, leading to a more rapid rate of skill acquisition and desired outcomes. Many case studies using TLP show improvements in sleep patterns, eye contact, social awareness and motor function.

TLP consists of an extensive series of high quality audio CDs that integrate specifically produced acoustic music, primarily classical, with innovative sound processing techniques that exercise the brain and auditory pathways. The programme was developed by a multi disciplinary team of experienced professionals from neuro-developmental, music, speech and language and medical backgrounds.

Listening to the CDs in the programme simply requires putting on a pair of headphones and listening to the music. For individuals with sensory challenges protocols can be used to develop headphone compliance and CDs are available to listen to through speakers.

The Listening Program is only available through a network of trained providers. TLP providers are primarily from the fields of speech and language therapy, occupational therapy, audiology, medicine or other health related fields. TLP is also available in a growing number of schools.

For more information contact
Learning Solutions, The Villa, 1 Hollingwood Lane, Bradford, West Yorkshire BD7 2RE
Tel: 01274 777250 | Fax: 01274 778754 | Email: info@learning-solutions.co.uk
www.advancedbrain.com | www.learning-solutions.co.uk

Massage therapy

Contributor: Jane Hider BPhil, RNIB Condover Hall School, Shropshire

When considering massage therapy with autistic children it must be recognised that all children respond differently, according to their stage of development or additional disabilities. What is enjoyed by one may not be appropriate for another, so a flexible approach and a patient understanding of the individual needs of the child are required if progress is to be achieved.

Touch and physical contact are basic mental, emotional and physical needs, giving feelings of security and self-awareness and contributing towards the development of self-esteem and human relationships. Massage is a structured way of catering for this innate need for loving touch. It is a useful skill for both parents and professionals to learn, to help with day-to-day frustrations and encourage an anxious child to become calm and responsive.

Massage is the 'art of touch' and a fundamental method of communication without language. Among the many physical benefits of massage are the relief of pain, improved circulation, better digestion and excretion and improved muscle tone. Nevertheless the social and emotional effects may be of primary concern to parents, carers and teachers.

Among the overall aims will be to:
- promote relaxation and the release of tension, thereby reducing anxiety and stress
- stimulate and develop language, using babble, singing or chanting and non-verbal communication through interaction and turntaking
- give choice and feeling of control
- overcome intolerance to touch and physical contact, and reduce self-harming behaviour
- improve sleep and overcome insomnia
- develop body-awareness and control and self-awareness
- be still and quiet and decrease hyperactivity
- reward good behaviour
- develop co-operation and relationships (bonding/trust/affection)
- encourage eye contact
- promote feelings of fun and pleasure (feelings of self worth).

Massage should take place in comfortable, safe surroundings free of disturbance or distractions. Some children show resistance initially but with sensitivity and perseverance grow to enjoy the experience.

Not all massage is relaxing. Some may dislike light stroking but enjoy deep pressure or percussive movements. Massage can be combined with more vigorous movements such as rocking, rolling, hugging, swinging and wriggling and viewed in the context of relationship play, fun and enjoyment.

For more information contact:
Jane Hider School of Natural Therapies, Sadhana, Farm Lane, All Stretton, Church Stretton, Shropshire SY6 6HR | Tel: 01694 723 468

Montessori techniques

Contributor: Montessori Centre International

The Montessori method is a child-centred approach to education. The key is the Prepared Environment where the child develops according to a unique individual pattern laid down by nature. The teacher acts as a director who provides a link between the child and the attractive scientifically-based educational materials.

A unique characteristic of the Prepared Environment is the freedom each child experiences to develop according to an inner guide. This means that each child is free to move, talk and choose appropriate work. The effect of this freedom is that the child achieves a balanced development with resulting spontaneous self-discipline. Of course there are limits to the child's freedom which are dictated by the social norms of the child's own culture.

Another unique characteristic of the Prepared Environment is the mixed ages in a Montessori class. The effect of mixing ages is that the children learn from each other and a social community develops.

An interesting feature of Montessori materials is that each exercise has a Control of Error or a point of interest which means that the child can self-correct. This leads to increasing independence and confidence.

Dr Montessori believed that education is a natural process where children learn by their own efforts in an environment which is carefully prepared to meet the child's needs. When these needs are met the child then develops according to nature. One result is a happy, resourceful, confident child who works independently with great eagerness. Another result is that the child is prepared for the next stage of development when a new prepared environment will meet the new emerging needs of the child. Dr Montessori had a cosmic vision and recognised the interdependence of all living things. This respect and appreciation for the work of the living and the dead is fostered in the Montessori class and the children come to know that they too can contribute to the well-being of others.

Here is the focus of the Montessori method: an education based on respect for the other. Dr Montessori believed that a new generation of peacemakers would result.

For more information contact
Barbara Isaacs, Montessori Centre International, 18 Balderton Street, London W1Y 1TG
Tel: 020 7493 0165 | Fax: 020 7629 7808 | Email: mci@montessori.ac.uk
www.montessori.ac.uk

Music therapy

Contributor: Jessica Curry BA (Hons) PGDip, Music educationalist and composer

Music therapy is the interactive use of music in a therapeutic setting and works on the basis that any person, no matter how disabled, can respond to music. There is growing evidence that many people with autism find music easier to process than speech.

The therapist aims to promote a sense of self and an awareness of others, not by teaching an instrument, but by using accessible instruments, listening and singing to encourage the participant to create their own form of communication and musical language.

The relationship and sense of trust between client and therapist is integral to the process and the sessions offer a safe space where feelings can be expressed and released through music. The therapist plays an active role and responds to and supports any musical communication from the participant. A great deal of the music is improvised, allowing the therapist to respond directly to the individual needs and moods of each client.

People with autism often dislike change. Music can help them to manage this as it combines progression and spontaneity with repetition and recognizable structures.

Music therapy is beneficial for all age groups but starting at an early age is recommended, as it may aid the development of key social and communication skills.

Music therapy's aims include but are not limited to:
- developing speech and language
- encouraging creativity
- increasing sense of self and of others
- promoting social and emotional development
- developing cognitive ability
- increasing sense of self-esteem and self-acceptance
- enhancing quality of life.

Further reading

Darnley-Smith, R. (2003) *Music therapy*. London: Sage Publications Ltd

Oldfield, A. (2006) *Interactive music therapy: a positive approach*. London: Jessica Kingsley Publishers

Bunt, L. (1994) *Music therapy: an art beyond words*. London: Routledge

*Curry, J. (2005) *Connections*. Portsmouth: Connections Music Company

Music therapy information sheet, available from National Autistic Society
Tel: 0845 070 4004 | www.autism.org.uk/a-z

Music therapy (continued)

Music therapy is now a state registered profession. Funding is usually provided by school, day centre or health authority budgets, or by private individuals.

For more information contact

British Society for Music Therapy
61 Church Hill Road, East Barnet, Hertfordshire, EN4 8SY
Tel: 020 8441 6226 | Email: info@bsmt.org | www.bsmt.org

Association of Professional Music Therapists
61 Church Hill Road, East Barnet, Hertfordshire, EN4 8SY
Tel: 020 8440 4153 | Email: APMToffice@aol.com | www.apmt.org

Nordoff-Robbins Music Therapy
2 Lissenden Gardens, London, NW5 1PQ
Tel: 020 7267 4496 | Email: admin@nordoff-robbins.org.uk | www.nordoff-robbins.org.uk

NAS EarlyBird Programme

Contributor: Jo Stevens, NAS EarlyBird Centre

The NAS EarlyBird Programme is a three month early intervention programme for parents of a pre-school child with a diagnosis of an autistic spectrum disorder. Six families at a time can participate in the programme, which combines group parent sessions with individual home visits when video feedback helps the parents to work with their child.

The programme offers a positive approach to living with a young child with autism. It aims to empower parents and give them confidence by providing information, explanation and practical strategies. Parents learn firstly to understand their child's autism; then how to develop social communication; and thirdly how to prevent problems and encourage appropriate behaviour. Parents find it helpful to share ideas and experience with other families who are 'in the same boat'.

The NAS EarlyBird Programme has been independently evaluated and was shown to reduce parental stress and encourage a more positive perception of their child's autism.

In 2003 an additional early years programme was developed based on the success of the EarlyBird pre-school programme. EarlyBird Plus aims to meet the needs of families whose child receives a later diagnosis (4-8 years). Parents attending EarlyBird Plus are encouraged to recruit a professional to attend the programme with them to encourage a consistent approach between home and school.

The EarlyBird Centre, in South Yorkshire, offers training in the licensed use of both EarlyBird and EarlyBird Plus to teams of autism experienced professionals who can then run the programme in their local area.

For more information contact
NAS EarlyBird Centre, 3 Victoria Crescent West, Barnsley, South Yorkshire, S75 2AE
Tel: 01226 779 218 | Fax: 01226 771 014 | Email: earlybird@nas.org.uk
www.autism.org.uk/earlybird

NAS *help!* Programme

Contributor: Andrew Powell, NAS *help!* Development Manager

In response to research which has clearly highlighted the importance of post diagnostic support for parents/carers, the NAS developed the help! programme. It has been running since 2001 and over 2600 families have attended programmes to date.

The NAS *help!* programme is a programme of information, advice and support for parents and carers of children, young people and adults, with a recent diagnosis of an autistic spectrum disorder. There is a great emphasis placed upon ensuring parents are aware of their rights and entitlements, and a similar emphasis on providing practical and clear up to date information. The NAS *help!* team are skilled communicators who ensure the programme is tailored to the needs of the parents in an informal but professional manner.

There are two main programmes currently run across the UK for parents and full time carers. These are the 20 hour programme and the One day programme.

The 20 hour programme is delivered across six day/evening sessions to include information on ASD, communication and behaviour support, educational issues, entitlements and benefits. The 20 hour programme is interactive and allows parents time to explore the various issues relating to their child. The 20 hour programme is for ten families – up to two members per family. In some locations a two day programme better serves the needs of families, so the programme can be run flexibly.

The one day programme is delivered on a single day and incorporates many of the key themes of the 20 hour programme. This programme is in presentation style but includes time for question and answer sessions. The programme is aimed at parents of 3-12 year olds, for up to 25 families.

Places for parents and carers are free.

help! has consistently received positive feedback. For example, analysis based on 400 parents who have attended the full twenty hour programme, indicated that 95 % of those parents believe that the programme has increased their knowledge of ASDs. Additionally parents have said that they value the opportunity to be with other families, share experiences and practical ideas to support their son/daughter with the diagnosis. Formal analysis of the programme has taken place in collaboration with Oxford University.

For more information contact
The NAS *help!* team runs programmes across England, Wales, Scotland and Northern Ireland and may be contacted via the NAS website or phone.
Alan Carman, The National Autistic Society, 2nd Floor, Church House, Church Road, Filton, Bristol BS34 7BD
Tel: 0117 974 8411 | Email: help.programme@nas.org.uk | www.autism.org.uk/help

National Autistic Society Schools

Contributor: Mike Collins, Head of Education Services, The National Autistic Society

Clientele

Specialist independent schools for statutory school age pupils with a diagnosis of autism. Schools take children up to at least 16 and usually until the end of their 19th year where appropriate.

Facilities

There are day and weekly boarding schools and 3 schools open 50/52 weeks per year. Staff pupil ratio is on average 1:2.

Aims

To provide a broad and balanced curriculum that takes account of the pupil's autism, learning needs and teaches independence and life-enhancing skills and experiences. Access to the National Curriculum (5-14 in Scotland) is incorporated into individually designed programmes.

Methods

Teaching is child centred and informed by an understanding of autism and the special educational needs arising from it. Structured teaching enables skills to be learnt in functional contexts and there is an emphasis on communication and personal and social education. Pupils are helped to conform to social norms and to gain access to as wide a curriculum as possible.

Direct teaching and therapy help remediate particular learning difficulties and increase individual understanding of the world. Wherever appropriate pupils are re-integrated into their local mainstream schools.

Outreach and Respite

A number of NAS schools have developed outreach and respite services for Local Authorities and maintained schools in their regions.

SPELL Framework

Over the past few years the educational approach of the NAS Schools (and adult services), has concentrated on specific programmes to reduce the effects of the impairment of imagination, communication and social skills that underlie autism. This is in addition to the generally accepted emphasis on structure, consistency, reduction of disturbing stimuli and a high degree of organisation.

SPELL

The approach addresses the needs for children with autism to have continuity and order in their lives. Children need to be able to predict events and their environment needs to be modified sufficiently to reduce anxiety.

It has been developed to overcome or reduce the disabling effects of autism by providing a broad and balanced curriculum which gives extra help in the area of impairments.

Structure helps with organisation and making sense of what can be a very confusing world. It can help provide a safer world by the removal or reduction of unexpected or unpredictable events.

Positive attitudes and appropriate expectations (not so high as to cause anxiety, and not so low as to cause boredom) aim to enhance the child's self-confidence and self esteem. We design education programmes which intervene in the child's autism aiming to maximise and build on strengths.

Empathy – seeing the world from children's unique viewpoint, and aiming to understand their perceptions demands empathy and uses the teacher's skills in designing a differential programme which starts from the position of the individual child.

Low arousal – the classroom and care setting needs to be calm and focused allowing opportunities for relaxation and relief of tension. Clutter and distraction may be inhibiting and a low arousal setting is likely to be most reassuring. We make use of physical education and a variety of relaxation techniques to maintain an ordered and harmonious atmosphere.

Our style is essentially non-confrontational and, through supported rehearsal, pupils are encouraged to try new and potentially aversive experiences thereby growing in confidence.

Links – it is vital that we communicate effectively with parents, other schools and agencies. In order to maximise the children's opportunities for inclusion in mainstream schools we access the National Curriculum and aim to maintain all the vital links with the community.

Evaluation

All schools are subject to inspection from OFSTED or HMI and Social Services. NAS Schools take part in the arms length accreditation scheme which is designed to focus on the quality of autism specific nature of the education offered to pupils.

For more information contact
The National Autistic Society, Services Division, Church House, Church Road, Filton, Bristol, BS34 7BD
Tel: 0117 974 8400 | www.autism.org.uk

Occupational therapy for people with autism

Contributor: Katja Michel, Occupational Therapist, Child and Adolescent Mental Health Service, Sandwell

Occupational therapy aims to enable people to participate in daily activities as independently and satisfactorily as possible, using meaningful activities as a means to achieve this. Occupational therapists work in a variety of settings and with a wide range of people, who for different reasons – physical or mental illness, learning disability, developmental disorders or other socio-environmental factors – struggle to fully participate in activities that life demands of them.

Due to the nature of autism, people with autism may come into contact with an occupational therapist at different stages of their life, when they find it difficult to engage in activities important for developing life skills, or for leading as independent a life as possible.

Hence, occupational therapists may see a person with autism in a child development centre, in schools or residential settings, in a mental health service etc. The therapist may use a variety of different approaches to support the person in overcoming the difficulties at hand. At all times, the approaches used should be person centred and treatment aims should be decided on together with the person/caregivers as much as possible.

The therapist may:

- assess the person's sensory processing skills and whether those are preventing him/her from participating in activities
- use behavioural strategies to help develop skills and adaptive behaviours
- use play to promote interaction and the development of social skills, and self expression
- use environmental adaptations to facilitate the person's ability to deal with everyday demands
- practice particular skills (ie motor skills, dressing, sequencing, kitchen skills, accessing community transports) to increase independence
- educate the person's environment (e.g. school staff, family, residential settings staff, work staff) on ways to facilitate participation in activities and help deal with demands of every day life
- help develop problem solving skills.

This list is by no means exhaustive, and the approaches used by occupational therapists can vary. Occupational therapists may also be involved in the diagnosis of autism.

For more information contact

College of Occupational Therapists, 106-114 Borough High Street, Southwark, London, SE1 1LB
Tel: 020 7357 6480 | www.cot.org.uk
and under their specialist sections: *Children, young people and families* or *Occupational therapists working with people with learning disabilities*

Osteopathy

Contributor: Kenneth McLean, Osteopath

Osteopathy is a manual therapy which aims to maintain the structural integrity of the whole body by optimising the body's ability t o heal itself.

There are a wide variety of treatment techniques including very gentle releasing techniques particularly suitable for children.

The osteopathic approach to autism generally addresses the neurological dysfunction found in the individual which may be responsible for the diagnosis of autism.

Cranio-sacral osteopathy is the most widely used osteopathic technique for the treatment of people with autism. Cranio-sacral osteopathy aims to improve the operating environment of the person's neurological system and as a result has a positive effect on the individual's behavioral and communication skills. This technique uses the osteopath's highly trained sense of touch (palpation) to identify and correct areas of dysfunction found throughout the body.

The effect of treatment may include improved social interaction, verbal skills and imaginative play. It should be noted however that with the absence of any widely used and recognised assessment tool for monitoring changes, these outcomes of treatment are subjective and very much based on feedback from parents and carers.

A study by Lavine (1999) suggests that cranial osteopathy as part of an integrated treatment approach can benefit the individual with autism.

Further reading

Fryman, V.A. (1998) *The Collected Papers of Viola M. Fryman D.O.,* edited by King, H.H. USA: The American Academy of Osteopathy.

Korth, S., (1995). Chronic Neurological Dysfunction In Children, *BOJ*, Vol. 15, p30

Lavine, L. (1999). *Osteopathic and Alternative Medicine Aspects of Autistic Spectrum Disorders.* www.autism99.org

Sandefur, R. and Adams, E., (1987). The Effect of Chiropractic Adjustments on the Behavior of Autistic Children: A Case Review. *ACA Journal of Chiropractic* Vol. 24(12), pp21-25

Upledger, J.E. and Vredevoogd, J. (1995). *Craniosacral Therapy*, 16th Edition. (Eastland Press). USA

Upledger, J.E., Vredevoogd, J.D., Retzlaff, E., Raynesford, A.K. and Howard, T.F. (1980). Autistic Children: Preliminary physiologic, structural and cranio sacral evaluations. *Journal of the American Osteopathic Association.* Vol.79 (12), pp123

Upledger, J.E., (1978). The Relationship Of Craniosacral Examination Findings In Grade School Children With Developmental Problems. *Journal of the Society of Osteopaths*, No.5, pp11-23

Osteopathy *(continued)*

Osteopathy should be seen as one aspect of a multi-therapeutic approach involving other health and care professionals aimed at supporting the specific needs of that individual. All osteopaths are registered with the General Osteopathic Council, the regulatory body for the profession.

For more information contact

General Osteopathic Council, 176 Tower Bridge Road, London SE1 3LU
Tel: 020 7357 6655 | www.osteopathy.org.uk

The Osteopathic Centre for Children, London: 15a Woodbridge Street, London EC1R 0ND
Tel: 020 7490 5510 | www.occ.uk.com

The Osteopathic Centre for Children,Manchester: Phoenix Mill, Piercey Street, Ancote, Manchester M4 7HY
Tel: 0161 277 9911

The British School of Osteopathy, 275 Borough High Street, London SE1 1JE
Tel: 020 7407 0222 | www.bso.ac.uk

PECS: The Picture Exchange Communication System

Contributor: Sue Baker, Director of Pyramid Educational Consultants UK

PECS offers a structured approach for developing early communication skills using pictures in a very different way from other picture-based systems. Originally developed in the USA for pre-school children with autism, PECS is now being successfully extended to a wider range of children with communication difficulties and also to older pupils. Since its introduction into the UK in 1996, PECS has become established worldwide as a significant new initiative in the field of autism.

PECS is based on a model that uses principles from applied behavioural analysis: looking at meaningful communication that is initiated by the child rather than being dependent on adult prompts. With PECS children are taught to exchange pictures for things they want in their environment. So, if they want a drink they will give a picture of a drink to an adult who responds with the requested item. With this 'exchange' format, skills that are critical to communication, such as approaching and interacting with a person and doing this spontaneously, are incorporated from the start.

The programme is divided into six phases. Starting with single pictures to communicate their needs, students are taught to discriminate between a variety of pictures and then to construct more complex sentences. The pictures and sentence strip are all stored in a portable communication book attached with Velcro so they can be easily removed when the student wants to communicate.

An exciting discovery is the number of children who develop speech after more than one year on the programme. The findings from the Delaware Autism Project provide grounds for optimism, with 76% of all children placed on PECS acquiring speech as either their sole communication system or augmented by a picture-based system. More recent studies confirm the gains in speech development following PECS training. PECS has also been used successfully for students who have developed speech but may not be using it communicatively.

Further reading:

Bondy A., and Frost L. (2002) *The Picture Exchange Communication System training manual.* Pyramid Educational Consultants, Inc.

Charlop-Christy, M.H. et al. (2002). Using the picture exchange communication system (PECS) with children with autism: assessment of PECS acquisition, speech, social-communicative behavior, and problem behavior. *Journal of Applied Behavior Analysis*, 35, 213-231

Ganz, J. and Simpson, R. (2004). Effects on communicative requesting and speech development of the Picture Exchange Communication System in children with characteristics of autism. Journal of Autism and Developmental Disabilities, 34, pp395-409

For more information contact
Pyramid Educational Consultants UK, Pavilion House, 6 Old Steine, Brighton BN1 1EJ
Website: www.pecs.org.uk

Person Centred Planning

Contributor: Lesley Waugh, NAS Person Centred Planning Manager

The Foundations of Person Centred Planning

"The term person centred planning refers to a family of approaches to organising and guiding community change in alliance with individuals involved in their services, their families and friends."
(O'Brien and Lovett)

Person Centred Planning means putting the person at the centre of their lives by listening and learning what they want from their lives now and for the future.

There are five key features to Person Centred Planning:
* The Person is at the Centre
* Family members friends and are partners in planning
* The plan shows what is important to the person now and for the future. It shows their strengths, gifts and talents and what supports they need
* The plan helps a person to be part of the community and helps the community to welcome them
* The plan is ongoing; everyone keeps on listening and learning to make things happen. The plan puts into action the things a person wants to get out of their life.

There are many different ways to plan with a person and these are examples of a few most commonly used:

MAPS – developed by Judith Snow, Jack Pearpoint and Marsha Frost

Planning **A**lternative **T**omorrows with **H**ope **(PATHS)** – developed by Marsha Frost, John O'Brien and Jack Pearpoint

Personal Futures Planning – developed by Beth Mount and John O'Brien

Essential Lifestyle Planning – developed by Michael Smull and Susan Burke-Harrison.

But person centred planning is really about an approach ensuring the person is at the centre of all aspects of their lives. Critically looking at how traditional service themes can be more led by the individual who uses the service; because people with an Autistic Spectrum Disorder need such individual supports it is very important that a person centred approach is used. It is rooted in the respect for the person, their rights and choices. It also focuses on what supports a person needs and how to keep them healthy and safe.

As a result of the governments White Paper 'Valuing People,' Person Centred Planning must be adhered to by the public sector. This is challenging to traditional services but not unachievable.

Further reading
John O'Brien(1987) *A little book of person centred planning-a guide to lifestyle planning.* Toronto: Inclusion Press
Beth Mount (1991) *Dare to Dream.* Toronto: Communities Books
John O'Brien (1991) *Person Centred Planning.* Toronto: Inclusion Press
Department of Health 'Valuing People' White Paper 2001

Websites
www.valuingpeople.gov.uk | www.circlesnetwork.org.uk | www.learningdisabilities.org.uk

Portage

Contributor: John Parry, National Portage Association

Portage is a home visiting educational service for pre-school children with additional support needs and their families. Since its introduction to the UK in 1976 there has been a big increase in the national provision and there are now 140 services registered with the National Portage Association (NPA).

The aim of Portage is to support the development of play, communication, relationships, learning and participation for young children within the family through weekly visits. The Portage home visitor works alongside parents offering practical help and ideas to encourage a child's emerging skills and address problematic situations.

Often the starting point of support is parents sharing with the home visitor their understanding of their child's gifts and support needs. Profiles or checklists can be used to identify strengths and goals for future learning. Parents take the lead in planning long term goals to ensure the relevance of Portage support.

Once a long-term plan has been made the focus of home visits shifts to deciding a weekly activity that the family can practice. The activities are based on play and everyday situations, providing fun and success for the child.

Portage offers a framework of support to which a family brings its own priorities. The curriculum was originally skills based but has evolved into a more flexible tool. Thus for children with autism an emphasis can be placed on social interaction and communication.

Many Portage services are trained in appropriate strategies such as PECS, TEACCH and Special Times. The NPA also offers training for parents and home visitors on working with children with complex social and communication difficulties.

The practical and emotional support that Portage offers is found to be an empowering influence by many families of children with additional support needs. However, Portage respects that the ordinary everyday things that families do are the most important experiences for any child.

For more information contact:
Brenda Paul, National Portage Association, PO Box 3075, Yeovil, Somerset BA21 3FB
Tel and fax: 01935 471 641 | E-mail: npa@portageuk.freeserve.co.uk | www.portage.org.uk

Programmes for adults with autistic spectrum disorders

Contributor: Carol Povey, Director of Adult Services, The National Autistic Society

Providing help to an adult with ASD requires a focus on the individual needs and wishes of that person and on the support needed to promote as full a life as possible.

We aim to reduce the disabling effects of autism and promote individual choice, independence and inclusion. The degree to which each of these Is achieved will depend on the individual characteristics of the person and on the quality of support given.

People with autism are particularly vulnerable to neglect, inappropriate treatment and social exclusion. To overcome this requires a positive approach that builds on strengths, discovers potential, enhances motivation and provides opportunity. It is not enough simply to offer protection.

No single solution will be appropriate. Just as the spectrum of autism is broad, so this is reflected in the range of interventions employed and the need for a person-centred approach.

Experience of working with people with autism suggests that a number of key features are important in reducing high levels of anxiety, enhancing quality of life, improving communication and motivation and developing skills.

Firstly, any approach must be based on a thorough assessment of **individual** attributes, needs and requirements. It should be **ethical** in that is does no harm and its effects can be assessed.

It should offer **structure** in making life more predictable, aiding teaching and communication and helping to promote choice and personal autonomy. Expectations and approaches are **positive** to build on strengths and develop potential and minimise regression due to low expectations or neglect. There must be an **empathy** for the way the individual sees the world; what interests or motivates them, what their strengths and interests are, what creates stress or anxiety, how they learn and how they think.

The environment should encompass **low arousal** approaches to ensure that as far as possible life is calm and organised, that aversive experiences are reduced or controlled.

A high level of consistency and continuity is essential and achieved through good communication and **links** between key supporters and the community. This also aids inclusion and quality of life options.

The approach is person centred and holistic and takes account of all aspects of the individual's life. These features will be reflected across a range of living and working environments, from residential services with high levels of support through to supported living and outreach options. Training and support for staff are essential to develop their expertise, reduce stress and promote enthusiasm.

Reflexology

Contributor: Ann Gillanders, Founder of the British School of Reflexology and Health Advisor for the Guild of Complementary Practitioners

Apart from the emotional changes in the child with autism, there are also connections with bowel disorders and a weakening of the gut wall. This allows foreign products to leak through the intestine into the lymph nodes which surround the bowel and consequently the blood stream, affecting brain function.

This is where the importance of holistic treatments comes into effect, reflexology being one. These treat the whole person, not the illness, and accept that the body, mind and spirit are involved when treating disease.

A toxic bowel creates a toxic blood stream. Our blood supply circulates through the entire body including the delicate structure of the brain.

Reflexology is a science that deals with the principal that there are reflexes in the feet which relate to all organs, functions and parts of the body.

Reflexology was used in Egypt some 2500 years ago along with many other forms of complementary therapies. When we hear complementary therapies being referred to as a new way of treating the body we should realise that it is the conventional forms of treatment which are 'new'. Complementary ways of treating the body in a gentle fashion have been around since the beginning of time.

By applying a deep pressure technique to the minute reflex points in the feet, a stimulation is created through the central nervous system. This is very powerful in relaxing the body, improving nerve and blood supply and generally detoxifying.

The greatest benefit of reflexology for the person with autism is an improvement to the functioning of the immune system. This aids an improvement in bowel function, detoxifying the body, particularly the liver, improving the function of the immune system and relaxing the body, mind and spirit.

Therefore the main areas that should be worked upon when treating the person with autism are the entire digestive system, the spleen, central nervous system, spine and brain.

However it is important to realise that, when using reflexology or any other form of complementary medicine, other aspects in improving health must be looked into: diet, exercise, and adequate hydration of the body are essential.

For more information contact
Ann Gillanders, 92 Sheering Road, Old Harlow, Essex CM17 0JW
Tel: 01279 429060 | Fax: 01279 445234 | Email: ann@footreflexology.com
www.footreflexology.com

Riding for the Disabled incorporating Carriage Driving

Contributor: Ed Bracher, Chief Executive, Riding for the Disabled Association

RDA's aim is simple: to provide disabled people with the opportunity to ride and/or carriage drive to benefit their health and wellbeing. In short, our aim is to make a difference to the quality of life of disabled people in a very special way.

We are a federation of over 500 Member Groups throughout the UK, each of which dispenses a unique therapy. Each week well over 24,300 children and adults enjoy the experience of riding or carriage driving, with opportunities to join in social activities, competitions or take a holiday. This brings a new dimension to necessarily restricted lives, encouraging independence and doing much to improve a wide range of medical conditions.

All this is made possible thanks to the commitment of more than 18,500 volunteers who regularly and cheerfully give their free time – and energy! – to ensure that RDA gives more than 400,000 rides and drives each year.

RDA is dedicated to ensuring that all our riders and drivers receive a high standard of professional tuition, tailored to their personal ambitions and capabilities. Our instructors work closely with health professionals to encourage every individual to aim for attainable goals – some modest, some far more ambitious. While competition plays a healthy part in RDA activities, our aim is to ensure that all our riders and drivers derive maximum personal benefit from a positive and enjoyable form of therapy.

Not all RDA Member Groups can offer all activities to everyone. Access to suitable facilities, availability of suitable horses, ponies and equipment and a substantial band of 'regular' volunteers are all crucial in the delivery of services. Our groups do their utmost to cater for every applicant. However, sometimes and in some locations restrictions on all these factors may mean that there is a waiting list.

For more information contact
RDA National Office, Lavinia Norfolk House, Avenue R, Stoneleigh Park, Warwickshire CV8 2LY
Tel: 0845 658 1082 | Fax: 0845 658 1083 | Email: info@rda.org.uk | www.rda.org.uk

Secretin

Contributor: Paul Shattock, Autism Research Unit, University of Sunderland

The hormone 'secretin' has been known since 1902. It probably has a number of functions within the body but is best known for its action in stimulating the pancreas to produce substances (bicarbonates and enzymes) which aid the process of digestion. It attracted considerable media attention in the mid 90s on the basis of one or two apparently spectacular reports.

The original product was probably highly impure and was made from the intestines of pigs. Totally synthetic sources were available but, anecdotally at least, the reported results were less impressive. For the past couple of years, a 'human' form of secretin has been biotechnologically produced and is currently being tested for safety as well as efficacy. Until then a number of products of variable composition and quality are available. The drug is normally administered by venous infusion requiring medical supervision and monitoring.

The drug was first employed because of its known role in stimulating the production of pancreatic enzymes. It was hypothesised that these enzymes would increase the rate of breakdown of peptides with biological activity, derived from foods, which could be responsible for the appearance of the symptoms of autism. The drug could however be affecting many other systems of the body. There are known to be receptors for secretin in the brain and it is involved in the immune system. The mechanisms which may be involved in the production of effects remain unclear but it is anticipated that these will be elucidated during the evaluation of the newer human form.

Unfortunately, the earlier highly encouraging results have not been produced in the trials so far conducted. However it is recognised that these trials were necessarily performed in a way that reflected actual practice in that a single dose was used whereas, in clinical practice, it is claimed that a number of doses spread out over five or six months are usually necessary to see beneficial results. There is evidence of physiological activity particularly in those children where severe gastro-intestinal problems have been noted but these have not necessarily been translated into worthwhile clinical improvements.

A homeopathic version is available given as sub-lingual drops. No formal studies have been performed but parental reports have been collected. Overall the reported effectiveness of the various forms of secretin are similar. Estimates suggest that in 30-40% of the cases some improvements are seen.

For more information contact
The Autism Research Unit, School of Health Sciences,
University of Sunderland, Sunderland 5RT 3SD
Tel: 0191 510 8922 | Fax: 0191 567 0420 | Email: aru@sunderland.ac.uk
http://osiris.sunderland.ac.uk/autism
See The Sunderland Protocol

Sensory difficulties and autism

Contributor: Olga Bogdashina, lecturer and writer on autism

Many people with autism have sensory problems. All senses might be affected: vision, hearing, touch, smell, taste, proprioception (body awareness) and vestibular system. Some people have severe sensory distortions while others may experience only mild but nevertheless confusing sensory difficulties. Non-verbal individuals usually have more severe sensitivities.

The commonest 'sensory differences' are the inability to filter out sensory information, fragmented perception, delayed processing, using one sensory channel at a time, hyper- and hypo-sensitivities, inconsistency of perception and vulnerability to sensory overload. These difficulties are often undetected. Many self-stimulatory behaviours – rocking, spinning, flapping their hands, tapping things, watching things spin, etc – may be involuntary strategies to cope with sensory overload, hyper- or hypo-sensitivity and distortions in the perception. The stereotyped activities can involve one or all senses. If we interpret these behaviours and identify their functions, we will be able to understand how the child perceives the world and help the child develop strategies to cope with these difficulties.

It is important to remember that people with autism have no control over their problems, as they are caused by neurological differences. They cannot change certain behaviours without specific help.

The unique characteristics of each person will require individual strategies and environmental adjustments. Moreover, a strategy may stop working as the child grows and need replacing by another to reflect changes in the person's abilities. Without treatment individuals with autism learn to compensate and use systems and strategies available to them, such as stereotyped behaviours, self-injury, aggression, tantrums and withdrawal.

As some sensory dysfunction is present in all individuals with autism, it helps parents of children with autism and professionals working with them to learn about sensory perceptual problems and ways to help them. The child's sensory perceptual profile is a good starting point for selection of methods and, probably, working out new ones, in order to address the individual needs of each particular child.

There are different treatments available to address sensory problems, eg, Auditory Integration Training (AIT), Irlen method, behavioural optometry, Sensory Integration Therapy (SIT). Treatment programmes that are appropriate and beneficial for one child may be painful and harmful for another.

Further reading

*Bogdashina, O. (2003) *Sensory perceptual issues in autism and Asperger syndrome: different sensory experiences – different perceptual worlds*. London: Jessica Kingsley Publishers

Sexuality and autistic spectrum disorders

Contributor: Lynne Moxon, Educational Psychologist

Parents and teachers need to teach children with ASD, from an early age, about their body, privacy, personal space, relationships and rules.

Many young people with Asperger syndrome (AS) want relationships but it is the lack of social understanding which can make it difficult to form relationships; the inability to look at things from another person's perspective can make relationships difficult to sustain. In some circumstances a person's sensory sensitivity can lead to problems with the intimate side of sex. Remember sex is not compulsory.

Sexuality encompasses more than sexual behaviour, it includes self-image, emotions, gender, values and attitudes but a young person needs to know about:

bodies
* women's and men's bodies
* naming of private parts, the differences and similarities
* menstruation and wet dreams.

Depending upon their level of understanding:

Sex – physical and practical aspects
* touch, public touch – where can you touch someone? – who can you hug?
* masturbation
* heterosexual activity – including consequences. Information on pregnancy
* same sex activity – including consequences.

Sexual health information
* contraception
* sexual health information.

Sex – social aspects:
* what does sex mean?
* why do people do it?
* how do we learn about sex?
* who can/can't we have sex with and why?
* right times and places – public and private
* keeping safe.

It is vital to teach friendship skills and as your child gets older so should his or her friends.

If people with an ASD are sexually active, what do they need to know?
* consent
* contraception
* saying no and coping with people saying no to them
* consequences (physical, emotional, social)
* can only be done with certain people in certain places (has rules).

Whilst sexuality and sexual behaviour are usually regarded as private, at times sexuality crosses from the private to the public sphere and the rules need to be understood otherwise the law will intervene.

Further reading

Melberg Schwier K. and Hingsburger D. (2000) *Sexuality: your sons and daughters with intellectual disabilities.* London: Jessica Kingsley Publishers

Newport, J. and Newport, M. (2002) *Autism, Asperger's and sexuality: puberty and beyond.* Texas: Future Horizons Inc.

*Willey, L.H. (ed) (2003) *Asperger syndrome and adolescence.* London: Jessica Kingsley Publishers

*Wrobel, M. (2003) *Taking care of myself.* Texas: Future Horizons Inc.

For more information contact
Videos: *Jason's private world; Kylie's private world; Jason and Kylie's private world.*
www.lifesupportproductions.co.uk | www.bbc.co.uk/relationships

Sensory integration therapy (SIT)

Contributor: Olga Bogdashina, author and lecturer

Sensory Integration Therapy (based on Delacato's theoretical foundation) was adopted by Ayres – to treat dysfunctional tactile, vestibular and proprioceptive senses. At present it is recognized that all the senses should be evaluated and worked at. The goal of SIT is helping the development of the nervous system's ability to process input in a more normal way.

There are several types of SIT: some are aimed at desensitizing the child to the stimuli they find painful, others to integrate the senses. They involve sensory activities aimed at raising the children's threshold for arousal.

A widely used concept of SIT is sensory diet, a programme of 'sensory exercises', designed to meet the needs of each child's nervous system. An occupational therapist teaches parents to use different techniques with the child at home and monitors the child's responsiveness to the strategies.

However, while recognising the difficulties of many children, these approaches still often address the symptoms and not the causes. Multi-sensory integration technique seeks to get people to use their senses simultaneously, in an integrated way. Though this approach does acknowledge that some people with autism work in 'mono' (using one sense at a time), it does not take into account what may cause this problem.

Some components of SIT, eg application of deep pressure and vestibular stimulation, may help some individuals with autism. It is easy to apply comforting deep pressure over large areas of the body to little children by placing them under large pillows or rolling them up in heavy gym mats. These procedures need to be done every day but not for hours on end. Depending on the children's anxiety level, some will need access to deep pressure and swinging throughout the day to calm down when they become overstimulated. Touch sensitivity can also be reduced by massaging the body and stroking with soft surgical brushes.

Supporters of SIT suggest that SI treatment can influence brain organization. However, until there is a sound theoretical foundation for the theory of SI and SIT, proper evaluation is unlikely.

Further reading

Ayres, A. J. (1979) *Sensory integration and the child.* Los Angeles: Western Psychological Services

*Bogdashina, O. (2003) *Sensory perceptual issues in autism: different sensory experiences – different perceptual worlds.* London: Jessica Kingsley Publishers

Delacato, C. (1974/1984) *The ultimate stranger: the autistic child.* Noveto, CA: Academic Therapy Publications

*Emmons, P. G. and Anderson, L. (2005) *Understanding sensory dysfunction: learning, development and sensory dysfunction in autism spectrum disorders, adhd, learning disabilities and bipolar disorder.* London: Jessica Kingsley Publishers

Yack, E., Aquilla, P. and Sutton, S. (2003) *Building bridges through sensory integration: therapy for children with autism and other pervasive developmental disorders.* Las Vegas: Sensory Resources

Social groups and social skills groups

Contributor: Anja Rutten, Head of Social Programmes and Befriending, The National Autistic Society

Many individuals at the high-functioning end of the autistic spectrum want to socialise and improve their social skills. Increasingly, social groups and social skills groups is seen as valuable opportunities for people on the spectrum to meet each other, and to learn about social skills which they might find useful for their life in the community.

There are many different ways to provide social opportunities. Any programme will need to be age-appropriate and tailor-made to suit the needs of the group and its individual members.

Social groups focus on providing people opportunities to participate more in mainstream leisure activities and although structured in their set-up and management, offer flexibility in what they provide, ranging from play groups or discussion groups with a fixed place to meet, to more physical activities such as rock climbing or ice skating. Whilst the emphasis is on being social and participating in activity, there are opportunities for learning of important skills such as how to build and maintain relationships.

Social skills groups are more focussed on attainment of skills and are therefore likely to be more structured. For young children social skills training is likely to revolve around turn-taking and sharing, whilst for older children friendship skills and keeping safe are important. Adolescents and adults may want to concentrate on transition into adult life, and the life skills necessary for participating in society.

Groups are most likely to benefit individuals at the higher end of the autistic spectrum, those who actively wish to socialise and individuals whose anxiety levels and behaviour are manageable in situations that involve several people at once.

For more information contact
PARIS (Public Autism Resource and Information Service) www.info.autism.org.uk is a searchable web-based service providing details of autism-related services and information, including social groups and social skills groups, developed by The National Autistic Society.

Social Stories™ and Social Articles™

Contributor: Marie Howley, Senior Lecturer, the University of Northampton

Social Stories™ and Social Articles™ have been developed by Carol Gray as a strategy for developing social understanding in individuals with autistic spectrum disorders (ASDs). The approach is based upon our understanding of differences in thinking and is underpinned by theoretical ideas such as lack of theory of mind and weak central coherence.

The social world is shared through a complex system of messages, often requiring non-verbal communication skills that remain an enigma, or 'hidden code', for many people with ASDs. Social Stories and Social Articles essentially present information about the social world that may be 'hidden' from the individual with an ASD.

The approach involves presenting information in a format that is most meaningful to the individual, resulting in individualised 'stories' or 'articles' that explain the 'what', 'when', 'how' and 'why' of a social event. Social Stories and Social Articles may be used to celebrate achievements or efforts, to prepare an individual for a new event and/or to suggest appropriate responses in a given situation. Gray provides detailed guidance on how to write Social Stories and Social Articles which comprise specific types of sentences written to a specific formula. Visual learning styles are also taken into account when personalising a 'story' or 'article'.

The principles of this approach include the need to gather information *before* attempting to write a Social Story or Social Article through reflective assessment, provision of missing information including the perspectives of others and indication of appropriate responses (and *why*). The resultant 'stories' or 'articles' should remain neutral and non-judgemental, guiding behaviour and providing insight to help to develop understanding of the social world. The approach can be combined effectively with other approaches such as 'Structured Teaching' of the TEACCH approach and 'circles of friends'.

Further reading

Gray C.A. (Ed) (1994) *The New Social Story Book,* Arlington: Future Horizons (available from Winslow in the UK)

Gray C.A. (1994) *Comic Strip Conversations*, Arlington: Future Horizons (available from Winslow in the UK)

*Gray C. (2002) *My social stories book*. London: Jessica Kingsley Publishers

*Howley, M. and Arnold, E. (2005) *Revealing the Hidden Social Code: Social Stories for People with Autistic Spectrum Disorders*. London: Jessica Kingsley Publishers

http://www.thegraycenter.org/

Speech and language therapy

Contributor: Joanna Lindley, SALT, Radlett Lodge NAS School

Communication and social interaction are two of the main areas in which people with an ASD show an impairment, so the Speech and Language Therapist (SALT) plays a key role in their assessment, diagnosis and intervention.

Assessment and diagnosis may be carried out by a multidisciplinary team of which the SALT is a team member or may be carried out individually by the SALT. The SALT's role in assessment and diagnosis is to evaluate the person's level of functioning in relation to developmental norms. This may include an assessment of the person's ability to use and understand spoken language, to communicate functionally using various different modes, their awareness of other people and their desire and ability to interact with others.

Intervention may take a variety of approaches.

Individual therapy sessions: this type if intervention is not usually appropriate due to the person with an ASD who has difficulty generalising across settings. However, if a SALT wants to work on the application of a specific skill, they might teach it in isolation before generalising it into different settings.

Parental input: approaches such as parent-child interaction, for example, More than Words (Hanen) or the NAS EarlyBird Programme, have proved particularly effective when working with pre-school children with an ASD. The goal of such programmes is to work with the parents to provide opportunities and teach strategies that will develop their child's communication.

Group sessions: musical interaction, attention and listening and intensive interactions sessions are often used with children with ASD. For the more able person with ASD who both uses and understands verbal language, social skills training may be appropriate. In this type of intervention a SALT teaches skills such as use and understanding of semantics, syntax, pragmatics, interpretation and inference.

Non-direct therapy: the SALT should ensure that the person with an ASD is provided with an environment which maximises their opportunities to develop all areas of their communication. This is likely to involve using visual means of communication such as photo/symbol timetables and, for those for whom it is appropriate, a communication system such as the PECS.

Further reading

*Barratt P. et al (2001) *Developing pupils' social communication skills.* London: David Fulton Publishers

For more information contact

Advisers on Autism, The Royal College of Speech and Language Therapists, 2 White Hart Yard, London SE1 1NX

Tel: 020 7378 1200 | Fax: 020 7403 7254 | Email: postmaster@rcslt.org www.rcslt.org

Supported Employment

Contributor: Gill Beech, Manager, NAS Prospects London

Prospects was established in 1994 by The National Autistic Society and was the first service of its kind to provide specialist help to people with autism and Asperger syndrome who were unemployed or needed support in work. The service currently operates in London, Glasgow, Sheffield, Manchester and Leeds.

Prospects aims to enable people with autism and Asperger syndrome to benefit from the range of employment and career opportunities available to non-disabled people.

Prospects recognises that job seekers with autism and Asperger syndrome have specific needs and also aims to address the needs of the individual. There are four main aspects to the Prospects service:
- employment training
- work experience
- job finding
- support in the work place.

Employment consultants with sound knowledge and experience of autism and Asperger syndrome provide training programmes consisting of small group workshops and one-to-one sessions which aim to address the specific barriers to finding work faced by the individual client.

Work experience with on-site support from an employment consultant is seen by Prospects as an effective way to assess the client's suitability for work and to identify support needs.

Employment consultants encourage clients to complete applications for job opportunities independently but are available to give assistance if needed. Advice is given to the interviewer prior to the interview and support is provided when the client attends the interview.

Employment consultants provide support for the person with autism, assisting with self organisation, time management and productivity. However, most time is spent on enabling the client to adopt the social norms of their particular working environment.

Further Reading

*Fausset, M. based on the experience of the NAS Prospects Employment Team (2005) *Employing people with Asperger syndrome: a practical guide.* London: The National Autistic Society

Howlin P. and Mawhood L. (1999) 'The outcome of a supported employment scheme for high-functioning adults with autism or Asperger syndrome,' *Autism 3* (3) 229-254. London: Sage Publications

Spence, G. and Penney, J. (2000) 'Practical strategies in the workplace: employment support workers at Prospects,' *The Autism Handbook* p113. London: The National Autistic Society
Harding R. (1999) 'Finding work,' *The Autism Handbook* p92. London: The National Autistic Society

Supported Employment *(continued)*

Employment consultants provide training and support to line managers and colleagues. This enables them to manage and support the employee with autism or Asperger syndrome once support from Prospects decreases.

For more information contact

Prospects London, Studio 8, The Ivories, 6-8 Northampton Street, London N1 2HY
Tel: 020 7704 7450 | Fax: 020 7359 9440 | Email: prospects-london@nas.org.uk

Prospects Glasgow, 1st Floor Central Chambers, 109 Hope Street, Glasgow G2 6LL
Tel: 0141 248 1725 | Fax: 0141 221 8118 | Email: prospects-glasgow@nas.org.uk

Prospects Manchester Anglo House, Chapel Road, Northenden, Manchester M22 4JN
Tel: 0161 998 0577 | Fax: 0161 945 3038 | Email: prospectsmanchester@nas.org.uk

Prospects Leeds Ground Floor, Coburg House, 2 St. Andrews Court, Burley Road, Leeds, LS3 1JY
Tel: 0113 236 6767 | Fax: 0113 236 6760 | Email: prospects-leeds@nas.org.uk

TEACCH (Treatment and Education of Autistic and related Communication-handicapped Children)

Contributor: Prof. Eric Schopler, Founder, Division TEACCH

TEACCH is the first comprehensive state wide programme in the United States, providing research and services across the age span throughout the state of North Carolina. It is located at the University of North Carolina School of Medicine with eight regional centres, each located in a city housing a branch of the state university system. There are also about 300 public school classrooms affiliated with TEACCH, using the TEACCH principles and procedures described below.

TEACCH also conducts extensive training programs, disseminating concepts and techniques implemented in the program. These have resulted in TEACCH replications in every continent around the globe.

The concepts and principles guiding both service and research are discussed in Schopler, E (1997) and Mesibov (1996).

They are as follows:

- understanding characteristics of autism from observing the child rather than from professional theories.
- optimum adaptation through two primary strategies: improving skills by means of structured education and modifying the environment to accommodate deficits
- parent-professional collaboration has been the cornerstone for developing services and for best helping individuals with autism
- assessment, using instruments developed at TEACCH for individualized educational programs
- structured teaching: children with autism can benefit most from structured teaching, emphasising the use of the visual modality.
- procedures are guided by theories grounded in child development, cognitive theory and behaviour theory.
- emphasis is placed on supporting and developing strengths and skills and using these for improving weaknesses
- holistic orientation: understanding and relating to the entire child regardless of specialised training and techniques applied. This is emphasised in TEACCH training
- continuity of community based service across the life span as needed.

Further reading

Schopler, E. (2000) 'International priorities for developing autism services via the TEACCH model' in *International journal of mental health,* 29 (1&2)

Schopler E. (1997) 'Implementation of TEACCH philosophy' in *Handbook of autism and pervasive developmental disorders.* 2nd Edition, pp 767-795. New York: John Wiley and Sons

Mesibov, G.B. (1996) 'Divison TEACCH: A collaborative model for service delivery, Training and research for people with autism' in M.C. Roberts (ed), *Model Programs in child and family mental health,* pp. 215-230. Mahawah. N.J.

TEACCH *Assessment Series* (2001) Austin, Texas: Pro-Ed

For more information see
www.teacch.com

Telephone helplines

Contributor: Caroline Hattersley, Head of Advice and Advocacy, The National Autistic Society

Telephone helplines vary in their remit, but can offer many services, varying from simply signposting to other organisations to offering in-depth advice, information and support or a listening ear. Some may offer advocacy and actively take on case work for enquirers. A majority of helpline services are free (other than for the price of the telephone call) and are confidential. Some are manned by trained volunteers, others by paid qualified staff.

The National Autistic Society offers several different national helpline services, all offering different types of support by telephone. All of these services have access to interpreters for callers whose first language is not English calling from within the UK.

The NAS Autism Helpline 0845 070 4004
(Mon- Fri, 10am – 4pm)
autismhelpline@nas.org.uk
Staffed by a trained team of advisers who have all worked with people with autism, the NAS Autism Helpline offers information, advice and support on all issues related to ASD to people with ASD or family members. The NAS Autism Helpline aims to empower callers by providing information from which families can make informed decisions about the future. The service is totally confidential. The NAS Autism Helpline also offers an email and written postal enquiry service.

NAS Information Centre 0845 070 4004
(Mon- Fri, 10am – 4pm) info@nas.org.uk

The NAS Information Centre provides a range of information services of interest to professionals and students including a free enquiry service, information packs for different professions and information sheets on specific topics.

NAS Advocacy for Education 0845 070 4002
(24 hour answer-phone service)
The NAS Advocacy for Education Service supports families of children with an ASD to access the education that they want. The service has two main facets: the Education Advice Line provides advice, information and support for any educational issue a child may be facing; the NAS Tribunal Support Scheme provides a case work service to families going through Special Educational Needs and Disability Tribunals. The service seeks to support and empower families to help themselves – providing assistance to those who need it but especially to those who cannot get help from other sources.

NAS Parent 2 Parent 0800 9 520 520
(24 hour answer-phone service)
parent2parent@nas.org.uk
The NAS Parent to Parent Line is a free, confidential telephone support service offered by volunteer parents to other parents of an adult or child with an ASD. All the parent volunteers share the determination to offer help and support to other parents.

For more information contact
Telephone Helpline Association
Tel: 0845 120 3767 | www.helplines.org.uk
A directory of helplines across the UK is available on their website.

Tomatis Method

Contributor: Patrick de la Roque, The Listening Centre

Dr A. Tomatis is an ear, nose and throat specialist in France who has pioneered auditory stimulation programmes for 50 years. The aim of the Method is to develop or re-establish communication when it has been impaired or lost on both emotional and physical levels. The Tomatis Method was not originally developed to treat autism but it has shown very encouraging results with this condition.

Dr Tomatis developed an electronic device that is a sort of working model of the real ear. It both filters and switches sounds on and off in such a way that the auditory system is 'forced' to respond in the ideal listening way. This listening device literally trains the auditory systems to become receptive and listen properly until the client's own ears can function properly without the device.

There are two very important muscles in the middle ear which work when we listen as opposed to just hearing sounds. These muscles are trained by the device to select the desired sounds and also to absorb loud sounds which are often so distressing to autistic children.

The Tomatis Method also reawakens the desire to communicate through music, using Mozart and Gregorian chants. The mother's voice is filtered as if heard in the womb. This is a symbolic way of reliving the developmental phases, leading to social language and hoping to restore a step that may have been missed because of physical or emotional difficulties.

These difficulties may be traumatic birth delivery; poor reaction to vaccinations or medicine; or other events in early life which may have impaired first attempts to communicate by switching off the listening.

The basic treatment consists of an initial 13 days followed by two 7 day sessions with two hours daily and a break of three to five weeks. Most children become more communicative, improve eye contact and become more aware and responsive. Sleep and appetite become more regular and hypersensitivity to sound is greatly reduced.

For more information contact:
The Listening Centre (Lewes) Ltd, The Maltings Studio, 16A Station Street, Lewes, East Sussex BN7 2DB
Tel: 01273 474 877 | Fax: 01273 487 500 | www.listeningcentre.co.uk

Yoga for children with autism spectrum disorders

Contributor: Stacey Betts, parent of a child with autism and author

Yoga techniques are designed to specifically address the symptoms of autism spectrum disorders. There is no cure for these disorders and their etiology is unknown at this time. However, parents and caregivers need options to help their children.

People with an ASD often have an impaired sensory system. A child with an autism spectrum disorder often feels heightened senses – hearing, touch, taste, seeing, smell. Their response to internal (eg feelings) and external stimuli (eg sounds) is also often heightened. A simple trip to the supermarket can lead to anxiety and even a meltdown.

Modified yoga techniques address problems with the sensory system and are designed to reduce maladaptive reactions to everyday events. Some children report that they feel more at ease and relaxed by using, for example, yogic breathing.

Yoga warming-up, strengthening, calming, and tension-releasing exercises are suitable for reducing many ASD coping mechanisms such as hand-flapping. They can also increase muscle tone, muscle strength and body awareness. Short and long yoga sequences can be tailored to fit the needs of the individual child.

Yoga for children with autism spectrum disorders is a fully illustrated book that combines our professional expertise with experience of parenting a child with Asperger syndrome. It offers a range of gentle and fun yoga positions and breathing techniques that are effective in dealing with the increased levels of anxiety, disorientation and tactile sensitivity often found in children with autism spectrum disorders.

Further reading
*Betts D. and S. (2006) *Yoga for children with autism spectrum disorders: a step-by-step guide for parents and caregivers.* London: Jessica Kingsley Publishers

For more information contact
Stacey Betts
Email: Sheysho@aol.com

Index

The National Autistic Society (NAS) publishes many helpful books on autism and Asperger syndrome. Here are a few titles

Autism: how to help your young child
Leicestershire County Council and Fosse
Health Trust
£10.99
www.autism.org.uk/pubs/recommended

*It can get better... dealing with common
behaviour problems in young autistic children*
Paul Dickinson and Liz Hannah
Illustrations by Steve Lockett
£5.00
www.autism.org.uk/pubs/recommended

*Asperger syndrome - practical strategies for
the classroom: a teacher's guide*
Leicester City Council and Leicestershire
County Council
£10.99
www.autism.org.uk/pubs/recommended

*Why does Chris do that?
Some suggestions regarding the cause and
management of the unusual behaviour of
children and adults with autism and
Asperger syndrome*
Tony Attwood
£6.00
www.autism.org.uk/pubs/general

*The undiscovered workforce: employing
people with Asperger syndrome: a
practical guide*
NAS Prospects Supported Employment Team
£8.00
www.autism.org.uk/pubs/work

Asperger syndrome: an overview
Christopher Gillberg and Stephan Ehlers
Translated from the Swedish by Charles
Olsen
£6.00
www.autism.org.uk/pubs/general

All these books and many more are available
from the NAS distributor:
Central Books Ltd
99 Wallis Road
London E9 5LN
Tel: 0845 458 9911
Fax: 0845 458 9912
Or order online @ www.autism.org.uk/pubs